Invitations to Play

Using play to build literacy skills in young learners

Anne Burke

Pembroke Publishers Limited

For Momma's artists Lily, Aidan, and Isabella
Always carry a purple crayon!

© 2019 Pembroke Publishers
538 Hood Road
Markham, Ontario, Canada L3R 3K9
www.pembrokepublishers.com

Distributed in the U.S. by Stenhouse Publishers
www.stenhouse.com

Library and Archives Canada Cataloguing in Publication

Burke, Anne M. (Anne Michelle),

[Ready to learn]
  Invitations to play : usi=ng play to build literacy skills in young learners / Anne
Burke.
Originally published under title: Ready to learn : using play to build literacy skills in
young learners.
Includes bibliographical references and index.
Issued in print and electronic formats.
ISBN 978-1-55138-336-1 (softcover).--ISBN 978-1-55138-936-3 (PDF)

  1. Reading (Primary). 2. Play. 3. Problem solving. I. Title: Ready to learn

LB1525.B86 2018   372.4   C2018-903299-5
                                    C2018-903300-2

Editor: Kate Revington
Cover Design: John Zehethofer
Typesetting: Jay Tee Graphics Ltd.

Printed and bound in Canada
9 8 7 6 5 4 3 2 1

Contents

Foreword

Observing children playing can be a fascinating way to watch human minds developing. Toddlers move from toy to toy, animating toys to become a part of their imaginary play world. Preschoolers use their imaginations, taking on make-believe tasks, imitating adults, playing side by side. Primary-grade children can focus more, building whole imaginary worlds both alone and together. And in every moment of play, all these children are learning.

Even in the simplest of activities, the youngest children are learning to use their senses to understand the world around them and how they can interact with it. Preschoolers are learning that they are social beings, that they have imagination, that they have ideas of their own. Older children are learning what their place in the world is; they are establishing the core ideas and values that they will hold throughout their lives. When humans are young, play is their work — the way they gather knowledge — and if we as educators and as parents watch and reflect on their activities, we can determine key elements of how and what they are learning.

This book is all about how children play and how, with thoughtful and subtle guidance, children's play can be an infinitely rewarding learning resource. Built on the work of the first edition, *Ready to Learn*, it draws on new research and ideas to create an even more exciting array of possibilities for educators and parents who want to utilize play as an effective resource.

Invitations to Play includes new text on the growing world of digital literacies, with a strong focus on how the playful use of digital tools can be used to enhance learning. It offers ways for parents and educators to choose apps that increase access to children's imaginary worlds and provide social opportunities, emphasizing creative collaboration.

The topic playful learning through music is expanded upon in new Chapter 9. *Invitations to Play* describes how children learn through musical explorations and offers educators numerous opportunities to help children develop sensory and collaborative knowledge through music. Educators will find out how to create unique and exciting music play centres, and do it using household items to create the instruments.

English language learners are an increasing part of our education system, something that this new edition recognizes well. Educators are given tools to engage ELL students through playful learning, to honor and build upon their home languages and ideas, and to help them find their way into English knowledge through social and collaborative interactions.

In this edition, Anne offers new and innovative ways to use play as scaffolding for later explorations in literacy. Indeed, this book is built on the idea of how invitations given by teachers can nurture multiple literacies through play-based experiences that celebrate what children know and can achieve when play is paired with their imaginative abilities. Preschool and early learning educators looking for ways to create foundations for reading and writing will find some here.

Anne has perfected the important balance between theory and instruction, and by so doing has created a guide which should provide an invaluable road map for educators and parents intent on exploring the bounteous world of playful learning.

David Booth
Professor Emeritus
OISE/University of Toronto

1

Using Invitations to Play to Build Literacy Foundations

Through their earliest years of play, children develop a substantial body of skills and knowledge. Along with their backpacks and snacks, this knowledge comes with them when they first enter a school. Most of them vaguely realize that attending school means they will learn to read and write, make new friends, and take their first real steps towards independence; however, all these experiences will be built on the foundations of everything they already know.

One of the biggest challenges that face educators is how to reconcile this early childhood knowledge with the formal education experience. A significant part of the early years' school curriculum is finding ways to build a base of knowledge on which skills may be taught. Programs, therefore, need to be designed in such a way that they address the needs of all children but are constructed in a manner that reflects the best knowledge and practices by which children learn.

And the best way for all young children to learn is through play.

Play as a Social Activity

This book is about play and the way that play can interact with early educational experiences. Pioneering psychologist Lev Vygotsky (2004) described *social play* as the way in which children come to understand rules, the rules that underlie all their social interactions. Early education expert Dr. Peter Gray (2008) describes it as the "means by which children develop their physical, intellectual, emotional, social, and moral capacities." All children's actions take on symbolic meaning, and through play, children build their understanding of the world around them. Play is also inherently social. It facilitates children's integration into peer groups and collaborative learning spaces. It is needed for children to assume other roles and viewpoints, and to establish close interpersonal communication. In other words, play and children's social interactions are irrevocably linked. As educators, we must understand that children do best when their social interactions are valued in the learning experience.

Conversely, enormous efforts and sums of money are being spent to prepare young children for their education. Some of this can be attributed to over-eager parenting; some of it is a creation of pop culture. An entire industry of online videos, expensive toys, and pre-preschools has sprung up to meet the perceived need to create an educational base for children's early school years.

As educators, we must ask ourselves fundamental questions about preparing young children for lifelong learning: What skills do they need? What teaching methods and learning theories best address how to build these foundational skills? How do we address the diversity of learners we encounter and bring needed cultural awareness to our classrooms? And, most important, how do we value and expand upon the home literacy experiences that children bring to the classroom door?

The Value of Home and Preschool Play

Children bring many different learning experiences to the classroom, but some have more experiences than others. Those who have been exposed to child-care settings or preschool already will have begun to build playful learning skills, to engage in learning how to learn. For children without this type of play-based foundation, reconciling their previous experiences to those of the classroom is more challenging. Explaining this difficulty becomes easier if we think about how children learn. Learning is a social phenomenon that takes place within a child's cultural world (Street, 2000). Children learn in many ways — through active participation in play, planned activities, observations and explorations they make, and imitation of adults and older children. Social interactions and explorations of how they understand their world are vital — and these are achieved through play (Branscombe, Burcham, Castle, & Surbeck, 2014).

Teachers today plan curriculum in key learning areas, building upon children's skills and social interactions to help them learn. The twofold goal in this text is to help educators understand the importance of play as a pedagogy for learning those early skills and to show them how to extend play through invitations to learners, so the learners can re-create the playful learning engagement they had before their formal arrival at school.

Although schools and teachers have struggled to find time for play in the face of academic agenda demands, most academics and educators recognize the value of play as a pedagogical tool. On a related note, parents are beginning to question homework policies, standardized testing, and the lack of socialization skills in children. Play is now understood to be foundational to young children's literacy building. In this text, I build on these new understandings and offer concrete and achievable ways for educators to extend invitations to play in all early years' learning.

My intention is to connect children's play to curricula and pedagogical practices. Teachers understand that children's learning at home scaffolds and connects to school learning — and much of a child's early life, up to and including the first years in school, is spent playing. This book offers a look at the benefits of engaging children in a pedagogy that honors what they know and prepares them for later years with a strong literacy foundation. The learning experiences provided by playing at home are of enormous value to what will happen later in the classroom; understanding this will enhance the roles of both teachers and parents. Play represents a huge opportunity to create a foundation for children's future literacy lives.

This book owes a heavy debt to my earlier title, *Ready to Learn*.

Emergent Literacy — Embedded in Social Practices

Emergent literacy, as termed by Marie Clay (1991), is the ongoing and developmental process of understanding and using language from birth until independence.

Typically, children from birth to eight years of age are in this phase of development. Emergent literacy begins with oral language, which is central to how children understand and communicate their needs and wants. Children establish language in order to connect words to specific actions and objects. Through their experimentation with language — the constructive process of engaging the world around them — and amid its constant feedback, children become competent "meaning makers" (Wells, 1999).

According to socio-cultural perspectives, children's home literacy engagements can be viewed as social practices situated within communities (Wenger, 1998). These social practices are ultimately the foundations of children's learning (Roskos & Christie, 2000). Through the early years of play and exploration, children acquire a substantial body of skills and knowledge (Hughes, 1991). Successful pedagogy recognizes that learning is not confined to the school and can neither begin nor end there. Embracing the valuable learning and language experiences that define children's first literacy engagements with the world is necessary for later success (Heath, 1983).

This book recognizes the fact that children participate in literacy engagements long before they can discriminate between letters or recognize the correspondences between letters and sounds (Clay, 1991). Auditory discrimination starts with the first sounds children hear, as children begin playing with sounds, letters, and eventually, words. Learning, beginning at birth, is based on what children are hearing in their homes and early environments. From their earliest moments, all children are active learners who construct knowledge and understandings within a series of age-related stages (Piaget, 1962).

The Skills versus Play Debate

Early childhood education is a challenging area. As society recognizes the importance of the early years in children's learning, there occurs much debate about the value of play in early literacy, as opposed to the skills model approach. The skills model is still dominant in North American educational strategies.

The U.S. educational strategy known as "Head Start" places huge value on early childhood skills acquisition. It promotes the social and cognitive growth of disadvantaged children through programs in education, nutrition, social needs, and health services to enrolled children and families. Canadian programs, such as ABC Head Start (Alberta), are based on a similar philosophy. In its *National Strategy for Early Literacy*, the Canadian Language and Literacy Research Network (2009) put a focus on skills, too, but stated its awareness of stakeholders' expanding definitions of literacy. The Network's report says that "literacy included not only reading and writing, but also speaking, viewing and representing, as well as what these mean to various social and cultural groups" (p. 11). Although this definition acknowledges literacy as a social and cultural practice, Canadian definitions of literacy remain skills based, as defined by the International Adult Literacy and Skills Survey and the Adult Literacy and Life Skills Survey. These surveys, conducted by the Organisation for Economic Co-operation and Development (OECD) and Statistics Canada, are quoted in the Network's *National Strategy for Early Literacy* (see p. 11).

One key recommendation of the Canadian Language and Literacy Research Network's report follows:

Children acquire fundamental literacy skills through an evidence-based instructional program that must include systematic, direct and explicit instruction, supporting the acquisition of essential alphabetic, code-breaking skills and development of strong oral language, vocabulary, grammar, fluency and comprehension skills. (p. 40)

This recommendation negates children's natural literacy acquisition in their own worlds and on their own terms. In fact, it holds children and play hostage in favor of a political and economic agenda. It ignores theoretical research on children's early literacy skills learning: children achieve language and literacy skills at higher levels when they experience rudimentary play scenarios and creativity in nurturing environments.

A lack of foundational skills for higher-order thinking points to the value of play. Despite a heavy emphasis on the 3 Rs in the Kindergarten to Grade 3 curriculum, educators and parents alike see that children often lack thinking skills such as how to make choices, generate solutions, and take risks.

Challenges of providing appropriate instruction

Generally, developing appropriate literacy instruction for the early years is a serious challenge. The programming is specialized and falls largely outside the university experiences of primary and elementary teachers. Although we know and understand that most children pass through stages of physical and intellectual growth, we also know that they do not reach each stage at the same time and that growth is highly individual (Clay, 1991; Piaget, 1962). Early identification of learning and other developmental difficulties is a challenge, but if met, can lead to interventions, providing more optimal pathways for successful first literacy experiences.

With a full academic agenda, it is difficult for teachers to return play to the curriculum; however, more research is advocating play as an effective pedagogical tool that centres learning in a holistic environment similar to a home environment. Including play as a pedagogical tool is especially a struggle when teachers lack experience in early years' classrooms. By using a natural form such as play, however, we can cultivate children's natural love for learning and build a base of knowledge that privileges the social and cultural contexts in which children learn, while focusing on the skills that schools value so much.

Issues that affect children's prospects as learners

High child poverty rates are still a huge concern, especially since child poverty studies suggest that family economics may lead to inequity later in life. As they grow up, children from poorer families often suffer health issues, missed opportunities, underemployment, and social exclusion out of proportion to their peers. All of this can be traced to a lack of early childhood intervention in education.

Research shows how early intervention using activities that engage children and challenge their young minds may affect some of their life path trajectories (Mustard, 2006). Other studies show that one quarter of Grade 1 students are at risk because of fewer resources in the home. Meanwhile, as a "Survey of Canadian Attitudes toward Learning" found, many Canadians think that early childhood learning should focus more on attitudes, such as fostering a positive attitude towards learning, than on school readiness (Canadian Council on Learning, 2007). All these considerations need to be part of a teacher education process, if it is to fully engage with the issues facing children preparing for school.

Challenges Facing Play as Learning

The role of play for children has come under much scrutiny by parents and educators. The word *play* once conjured up visions of children engaged in spontaneous thought, movement, and expression. Historically, it evoked images of carefree children running in fields, playing games, and climbing trees. Unfortunately, it has acquired another connotation: that of time wasted and educational opportunities lost.

Reasons related to work help explain why play has been relegated to spaces outside curriculum. In a crowded world, playtime — or, to use a favorite term of parents, *quality time* — is often something left when the "real" work has been done. This dichotomy between work and play is formalized in the workplace. Play is not considered to be a productive measure or preparation for the world of work; this sort of office and organizational thinking is too frequently transferred to the home and classroom.

Many early-grade teachers often struggle under the weight of school and societal expectations. They think they ought to keep children almost always engaged in serious learning tasks: tasks that, in some obvious fashion, prepare them for gainful achievement. This rarely stated (but commonly held) perspective holds that, outside the playground, play has no real place in our schools. On one hand, schools put great importance on play as a socialization activity; on the other, they often confine it to physical education classes, lunch break, and recess. Furthermore, although much research shows intricate connections between play and skills development, it is difficult for parents and educators to see how learning gained through play is transferable to work-related skills. Unfortunately, some types of play do not fit well within the confines of the structured and expected behaviors of children in school.

For too long, many educators and parents have undervalued play and viewed it only as a playground or physical education class activity.

Play as a form of learning is subject to other challenges. The outcomes of play are difficult to quantify. Educators also tend to have set ideas about good play and bad play. Meanwhile, the media, popular culture, and overt child consumerism have pushed the boundaries of childhood outwards, towards mimicking the real-life experiences of adults.

Nonetheless, a playful curriculum has much value. Creative in form and innovative in ideas, it produces children who show resilience in the face of change and can share divergent thinking about the everyday nuances that define their lives. The ability to explore and confront such changes prepares children for later experiences where changing patterns in life are becoming the norm. *Crisis in the Kindergarten: Why Children Need to Play in School* is a 2009 report from the Alliance for Childhood by directors Edward Miller and Joan Almon. The U.S. report makes this argument: "Creative play that children can control is central to their physical, emotional, and cognitive growth. It contributes to their language development, social skills, and problem-solving capacities, and lays an essential foundation for later academic learning" (p. 63).

The literature written on play is also very supportive of its role in the literacy development of the child. Several researchers (see Dyson, 2003; Edminston, 2007; Gregory, Long, & Volk, 2005; Hall, 2000; and Morrow & Rand, 1991) report that literacy engagements for children are enriched through pretend play. Jane Hewes (2006) says, "In play children explore and test the edges of what they know, where they begin to understand what it feels like to reach for something new, and to achieve something originally impossible, even unimaginable" (p. 33). Seeing the rightful placement of play as a pedagogy that responds to and addresses early literacy and numeracy skills is a return to the natural way in which young children learn.

Play as It Relates to Curriculum Planning

If we agree that play is fundamental to the development and educational success of our students, then the challenge becomes how to bring play into a formalized curriculum, where skills are seen as the focus for future achievement. The following are aspects of play that need to be considered in relationship to (and with) curriculum planning for the early grades.

- Children learn in a holistic environment, one that encourages learning through speaking, listening, creative thinking, and moving, all of which are conducive to play-based exercises.
- Learning should be a hands-on experience, with classroom learning centres that develop independent thinking, learning, and other initiatives driven by children's desire to learn.
- Children need to learn in spaces that acknowledge and build on the socio-cultural dimensions of home and family that they bring with them to school.
- Since children learn and grow at different rates, educators must develop programs that are responsive to every child's needs and that exemplify learning through play as a pedagogy that provides equity. Teachers must be mindful of their students' needs.
- Effective teaching practice requires having a philosophy that places play as important to learning and understanding.

Preparing to facilitate play

Play can find a space in classrooms where the teacher has mastered such skills as keenly observing learning moments, sharing and communicating to find children's voices, and using play to help children connect their feelings and thoughts with words. Teaching children how to freely communicate their thoughts and feelings to others is needed if, ultimately, they are to interact with their world of learning. To successfully introduce or encourage play in their classrooms, teachers need to do the following:

- model attitudes that recognize and use play in the curriculum as a learning pedagogy
- gain an understanding of the importance of play and its vital relationship to learning
- understand how to include appropriate play experiences for young children
- learn how to contribute to play without controlling children's exploration
- understand how to encourage certain learning goals in play when working alongside children
- recognize the importance of socio-dramatic play in the construction of children's identities
- create spaces for and categorize play for learning

Offering enriching opportunities

Kindergarten teacher Karen Jennings makes use of these materials, as described. This table is derived from *The Right Stuff for Children Birth to 8* by Martha B. Bronson (1995, pp. 120–121).

During the primary years, children benefit from complex play invitations when paired with materials that enrich play opportunities. The importance of the materials in the classroom environment should not be overlooked. The choice of materials and the equipment chosen for the classroom should optimize learning opportunities. The suggested materials in the table (pages 14 to 15) foster creativity, musicality, critical thinking skills, understanding of math concepts, and problem-solving skills. They also aid physical achievement.

Play as Children's Work

At its simplest, play is children's work and the way in which children make sense of their formative world (Piaget, 1962). Children's play is used for different functions, such as social engagement, symbolic expression, and motor activity. All these forms of play show traces of the identities of children and may be an expression of power within themselves and how they communicate with others. Essentially, play is what children do in their world and it is fun. Through it, we see the development of children's cognitive skills, such as fine and gross motor skills; an orientation to their environment; and skills of socialization to play out with others. In many ways, play is the foundation upon which these types of skills for life are built.

The building blocks for life that are found in play-based activities show the intricate link between play and life. Child play provides opportunities to engage hildren through a performance of life: one that can be experienced in a safe environment. Language and communication skills, problem solving, and the use of critical thinking strategies are all needed. Play is a chance to practise these skills that are so much a part of a child's life (Bruner, 1978).

Socio-play Materials	
Social and Fantasy Play	**Dolls:** – washable, rubber/vinyl baby dolls (with culturally relevant features and skin tones) – accessories (culturally relevant) for caretaking, feeding, diapering, and sleeping – smaller people figures for use with blocks or construction materials **Role-play materials:** – materials for creating and practising real-life activities – play money with correct denominations – book- and letter-creating materials **Puppets:** – puppets that represent familiar and fantasy figures for acting out stories (children can also create their own) – simple puppet theatre: children can construct theatre and create props and scenery **Stuffed toys/play animals:** – realistic rubber, wood, or vinyl animals to incorporate into scenes and models or that show characteristics of animals being studied (such as reptiles and dinosaurs) **Play scenes:** – small people/animal figures and supporting materials with which to construct fantasy scenes or models related to curriculum themes **Transportation toys:** – small, exact (metal) replicas preferred by children of this age range are not usually used in school settings, but more generic small models are useful – construction or workbench materials for children to use to make models of forms of transportation
Exploration and Mastery Play	**Construction materials:** – a large number of varied materials for detailed construction and for creating models (can use metal parts and tiny nuts and bolts) **Puzzles:** – three-dimensional puzzles – jigsaw puzzles (50–100 pieces) **Pattern-making materials:** – mosaic tiles, geometric puzzles for creating permanent designs (art and craft materials) **Dressing, lacing, stringing materials:** – bead-stringing, braiding, weaving, spool-knitting, and sewing materials now used in arts and crafts **Specific skill-development materials:** – printing materials, typewriters, materials for making books – math manipulatives, fraction and geometric materials – measuring materials: balance scales, rulers, graded cups for liquids – science materials: prism, magnifying materials, stethoscope – natural materials to examine and classify – plants and animals to study and care for – computer programs for language arts, number, and concept development and for problem-solving activities

	Games: – simple card and board games – word, reading, and spelling games – guessing games – memory games (Concentration) – number and counting games (dominoes, Parcheesi) – beginning strategy games (checkers, Chinese checkers) **Books:** – books at a variety of difficulty levels for children to read – storybooks for reading aloud – poetry, rhymes, humorous books, adventure books, myths – books made by children
Music, Art, and Movement Play	**Art and craft materials:** – a large variety of crayons, markers, colored pencils, art chalks, and pastels (many colors) – paintbrushes of various sizes – a variety of paints, including watercolors – a variety of art papers for drawing, tracing, painting – regular scissors – pastes and glues (nontoxic) – collage materials – clay – craft materials, such as simple looms, leather for sewing and braiding, papier mâché, plaster of Paris, and small beads for jewellery making **Musical instruments:** – real instruments, such as recorders (sometimes used for group lessons in school setting) – a wider range of instruments for children to explore (borrowed or brought in by parents or special guests)
Gross Motor Play	**Balls and sports equipment:** – youth or standard-sized balls and equipment for beginning team play (e.g., kickball, baseball) – materials for target practice (to practise skills) **Outdoor and gym equipment:** – complex climbing structures, such as those appropriate for age five (including ropes, ladders, hanging bars, rings)

Lenses through which to examine play

The concept of play is both complex and dynamic. Widely differing viewpoints have emerged about young children and play. Young children's language and development is not a fixed field, and the varying issues surrounding play are constantly being re-examined through different lenses.

Play has been studied only in quite recent times. Before the 20th century, most children not from wealthy families spent their time either in an educational system or in work to help support their families. Whatever else they did was of little interest to the adult world. At the turn of the 20th century, the lives of children began to be examined in earnest, in hopes of turning children into better adults. Psychoanalytical perspectives on play were initially based on the work of Sigmund Freud and then later looked at and revised by others. In Freud's view, child's play offered glimpses into the internal and external development of the id and the ego, with various sexual stages demonstrated along the way.

Erik Erickson (1963) believed that children's engagement with play developed their self-esteem, thereby giving children mastery over their thoughts. He reached these conclusions by studying children's body movements, the representational forms children used to communicate their thoughts. Erickson came to realize that children naturally interconnect what they wish to communicate with their activities and social play. In short, children explore challenging play scenarios as a way to respond to the world.

The confidence gained in finding power over a situation that, in the real world, may be too difficult to confront, can be very empowering to children. Role-playing a teacher or a parent who has authority gives the child a chance to work out different viewpoints, new ideas, or even fantasies of being someone else. Children's play is complex because it mirrors the fantasy as well as the reality of some children's lives. It is played out through an experiential process that sometimes is encouraging to self but also confronts the anxiety and helplessness that may characterize children's lives.

From the work of Russian psychologist Lev Vygotsky (2004), we have learned that children individually create knowledge about the world through the interactivity that surrounds, characterizes, and defines their world when they play. Most of us can remember instances where this principle came into being. For example, I once visited a Kindergarten class where some of the children were playmaking around the fable of the tortoise and the hare. When someone asked where the race could take place, one child suggested the street where the local Santa Claus parade was held. Another child countered with his own residential cul-de-sac. A third child recommended a market area in Bombay often mentioned by older family members. When playing, the children were incorporating their implicit cultural values. Although these children came from culturally diverse backgrounds, they each had developed their own mental schemas and were drawing on their experiences to interact and play with others.

From a socio-cultural perspective, play, as experienced as a social interaction, is the first and most important encounter with the knowledge from the child's world. It is how children share their cultural values and beliefs, which are embedded in the scenarios they create. Spontaneous play activities found in childhood show the greatest competencies of children. Exploration of their worlds through the freedom of play leads to new ideas and behaviors to be tried out. These play-based performances show how children develop their understandings of how to reach out to embrace new skills.

The difference between what a child can do alone and what he or she can do in an environment with a supportive individual is called the "zone of proximal development" (Vygotsky, 1978). New skills and development are shown by the child in the presence of another who works to "scaffold" the child's efforts in learning. After acquiring this expertise, the child makes the performance of such skills a part of his or her repertoire.

Psychologist Jean Piaget studied children's behavior extensively throughout his life. Piaget (1962) felt that children create their knowledge of the world through individual interactions with people, objects, and materials; this, in turn, leads to a sharing of knowledge based on the children's perspectives. Through play, children test new ideas and learn to regulate their behavior. Piaget focused on two important outcomes of play: first, that play brings joy and satisfaction; second, that learning is produced through the interaction of play. According to his cognitive-developmental stance, children can learn to regulate their behavior to show new learning and understanding through use of the many forms of play. Piaget's common-sense views would probably reflect those of many parents and children. His theories about children's development have influenced the entire makeup of elementary school curricula.

According to social learning theorist Albert Bandura (1977), children learn social behavior not only through direct experience with an event, but also through observation of what happens and how others act within that event. Any educator will have seen this theory in action, for example, when a child imitates or copies another behavior in anticipation of receiving a reward for that behavior. Teachers often use this behavior as a classroom tool through a compliment/reward system, wherein children learn to follow other children based on the teacher's rewarding of positive efforts.

The Value of Play

Playmaking brings children a greater awareness and understanding of the world in which they live. Sutton-Smith (1971) describes play as an inquiry process that consists of four ways of *knowing*: (1) exploration, (2) testing, (3) imitation, and (4) construction. When children play, they construct an understanding of what the world means for them in their own cultural milieu, using these four ways, together or individually, to create their knowledge base.

By way of illustration, in preparing the material for this text, I watched a group of children devise an imaginary TV show about cooking, which involved creating recipes through use of symbolic play and representational objects. Through the role play, they shared their understanding of how things are interconnected. For example, they chose brand-name products found in their homes for ingredients in their recipes, discussed the grocery stores where their families shopped, and used cooking vocabulary, such as calling a spoon for serving soup "a ladle." When something like this occurs naturally during play, it is a great teaching opportunity, a moment to introduce new vocabulary and make connections to the children's real-world experiences.

This exploration of their environment through play shows how children imitate people who are in their lives. Through engagement with their peers, the children showed an understanding of the narrative of a cooking show and of the actions of peers in varying contributory roles. When a play narrative is freely explored, we can see how the play of the children changes constantly, illustrating their ways of knowing in areas of exploring, predicting, constructing new meaning, and testing out that meaning with further exploration.

Play enthusiast David Elkind (2001) feels that play unifies children's mental, psychological, and socio-emotional development. Elkind argues that, in the early years, the function of play is to give children the means for developing a sense of competency, especially a sense of competency of the whole self. When children successfully complete a task or action, they feel good — and this is what we want to focus on in building confidence in young children through play. Play has the ability to unify and bring all of these aspects together in the learning development moment.

In summary, play is an important medium to children's social, emotional, and cognitive development (Piaget, 1962). When children play, we see how this holistic engagement invites creative expression: play episodes call for an improvisation of scenarios that show how children must be open to giving and taking ideas during the playmaking. Such playmaking fully involves their imaginations in how they develop symbolic representations of the objects and spaces to satisfy the needs of the play. Children should be encouraged to think and explore options with flexibility. They need to be able to get across their ideas to their peers, as well as to understand how they can extend and explore further a given idea.

Play also plays a key role in the development of social confidence. By its collective nature, it requires interaction with others, and the regulation and control over emotions. To take on new roles in play situations, children must share and understand the rules of turn-taking and resolving problems. Interaction and play episodes will naturally bring forth arguments so children will have to learn to respect others' ideas, cooperate with one another, and build the foundations of early friendship. These social skills are much needed in the world of Kindergarten but also in the world beyond it.

Physical play has a developmental role, too. It develops large and small motor skills, the idea of safety's role in self-preservation, an understanding of the body's nutrition needs, and trust in the ability to make decisions. Play is vital to all these processes.

How Children Feel about Playing

Most of the comments given below come from the 2018 Adventure into Sport: Evaluation Report conducted by Play England, an organization that works to ensure that policy makers, parents, and the public recognize the importance of play. As one play worker observed: "When kids are playing there isn't a right or wrong . . . You don't have to be the best and the fastest, if you want to do it and have fun with it, great, and if you don't just leave it, . . . having that affordance and freedom really set out to you helps. Taking away that pressure" (p. 28).

Children described what they felt about play in these terms:

- "It makes you stronger, healthier."
- "I feel like when I come to the big swing, I feel better about myself because I can meet more friends."
- "Dodgeball, I enjoyed the most because it was competitive, friendly competitive everyone got to do it as well."
- "When I first came here, I was scared of the jumping tower, to jump off the top one, and I started to try it and I got better at it, now I can jump off of it."
- "What I like to do is mostly play on the pirate ship, I don't know about you, but I always wanted to be a pirate. I still love Pirates of the Caribbean." (pp. 32–33)

The next set of quotations about playing come from a 2018 video created by Play Wales on Playing and Hanging Out:

- "I like playing around and climbing up trees or playing tag with my mates. Just anything really as long as it's fun."
- "If there's no playing, there's no way to find out what's around you really. If you don't play, you're sitting around bored."

- "Playing helps you think really."
- "Play is fun."
- "Play is like a place where you can hang around with your friends and meet new people and have fun and enjoy yourself."
- "Play is better without adults. Because there is no rules. Adults force you around and give you time outs."
- "You make new friends easily."

Sources: Play England (2018); Play Wales (2018).

Come Play with Me: Types of Play

Sara Smilansky (1968) carried out an important study with preschool children in both the United States and Israel. All the children came from a lower socio-economic background. Her observations of children's play are given under the following categories: functional play; constructive play; symbolic, or dramatic play; rough and tumble play; and games with rules.

Functional play

Functional play is sometimes known as "practice play." Children create, become, and enter imaginary worlds as they choose to find ways of exploring episodes that mimic real life. I recall watching my son pretending to start an imaginary car with Mommy's keys, a game of which he never tired. Activities like these can be practised repeatedly. You may have heard parents comment about other such repetitive activities, pointing out that their child "does that over and over again." The play, in this case, is a learning opportunity for the child. Focused within such a play scenario, the child pretending to start Mommy's car is refining motor skills while practising an action that imitates one in the world of adults.

As children learn new skills, even ones as basic as running and jumping, practice allows them to perfect these skills. Hopping on one foot around a hopscotch plot shows how they are developing balance, while trying to do leg splits shows how they build flexibility. Many parents grow tired of the constant "look at me" refrain while their children demonstrate some minor physical achievement; however, the children are demonstrating how practice play leads to self-confidence, success, and control over their bodies and self.

Functional play example: *A child named Sarah practises writing her name, gripping the pencil with a fierce concentration as she controls the direction of the S. Eventually, she fills up the page from top to bottom with versions of the letter. This type of writing is not intended for communication, and the writing will not be shared with others. Its purpose is the pleasure of the practice.*

Other types of functional play relate to memory. Listening to children sing the same verse of a song over and over may be dull for the educator, but for the children, it becomes a part of their recall, helping with intellectual sequencing and serialization (memorization). An understanding of the song's meaning, along with ways in which they refine, practise, and succeed with it, develops children's abilities.

Constructive play

Constructive play involves making, building, and creating based on ideas. It is the manipulation of objects, with the goal of creating something new or imagined, as well as putting things together to make representations of reality. Constructive play, such as digging a hole to China and imagining the possibilities of adventure upon arrival, is a form of departure from the world; it bridges new understanding. Through the engagement of teachers observing and helping them to critically question their assumptions, children may extend their language and conceptual understandings of the world in which they live.

Constructive play — An example of teacher scaffolding: *The teacher produced a large bowl of beads for her Kindergarten class. She demonstrated how to string the beads onto a piece of twine and then explained how she liked to make a pattern of one red bead, one blue, and one green for a necklace. She cut and knotted some string for the children and then left them to their own devices. Two of the girls made recognizable necklaces, with the beads in carefully arranged patterns. One boy produced a string with all the beads the same color. Another boy used the beads to create an imitation snake on the tabletop. The last boy just played with the beads, filling and emptying the bowl, pretending they were bits of cereal or noodles and he was preparing a meal. Eventually, the teacher spoke to each child, reinforcing the lesson that each had learned through constructive play — patterns, creativity, or imitation.*

Moments like these offer wonderful opportunities for teaching. Concepts from mathematics, art, or social studies can be introduced into the play, all while children continue to explore, unaware of the educational addition.

Symbolic, or dramatic, play

The art of dramatic play happens when children engage in symbolic representation, using objects to imitate other activities. For example, using a spoon as a brush, children may move from role-playing a mother making soup to becoming a hairdresser in a salon. The symbolic representation of various people and literacy events played out show how children's worlds are developed (Bruner, 1996). When the play corresponds to ideas about how to act in our world, it becomes known as "socio-dramatic play." (See Chapter 7 for more information on symbolic play.)

Symbolic play example: *In the house corner, Abigail and Teeba have found themselves at a loss because there was no plastic food for them to use in their symbolic play of a picnic. While busily placing plastic plates and cups in a picnic basket, they discovered that there was no plastic food in the bins because it was being cleaned. They realized that they had to use what was on hand to continue to play . . .*

Abigail opened her hand to Teeba, revealing small, plastic-wheel construction pieces she had found in the bottom of one of the bins.

"Look. Let's use these," she said. "They can be our food. See, the shape is like a wheel, like the pasta we have at home."

Abigail picked up a yellow block and said, "This is the cheese."

Rough and tumble play

Combining aspects of both functional play and dramatic play, this form of play accompanies the pretend play. Specific not just to boys, it is often seen as wrestling or as pretending to be someone else, such as a superhero. Playing heroes and victims, children learn to negotiate the roles and choices that they make in real life.

Rough and Tumble Play — Superhero Time

Carol Sanchos, an experienced Grade 1 teacher in a suburban elementary school, is well aware of the attraction little boys have for rough and tumble play, which is often at odds with classroom conventions. During a unit on heroes, she noted how many of the boys were fascinated by superheroes. She decided to build on this, using play-based scenarios, to encourage some of the more reluctant writers and classroom participants.

One day she suggested to the class that the children each create a superhero. They had to pick a name, a power, and a special clothing item the hero had to wear. The only rule was that the superhero's power could not be violent. Many of the children were enthusiastic. Carol did not discourage the discussion that ensued and, instead, quietly monitored it.

Daniel: My superhero is going to have a mask. He's going to be invisible.

Jeremy: Cool. My guy . . . my guy . . . my guy is gonna look like a rock star.

Daniel: What's his power going to be?

Jeremy: He'll be invisible, too . . . No, he is going to be able to turn to rubber!

Kate: My hero will be named Willow and will be able to turn into a horse . . . see, she has yellow hair and ribbons, just like me.

The project was a huge success, as the children's efforts to draw and create and explore their superheroes' powers through socio-dramatic play spilled over into lunch and play times. Later, the class constructed a series of simple comic-book frames, based on the adventures of a hero they created together.

Games with rules

Playing with rules means that the child is expected to acknowledge and accept the rules and conform to the structure of the play. The play is, therefore, controlled by others. Children struggle with these types of games, as their natural desire is to come up with their own rules. Playing by the rules and conforming to the expectations of a game can be difficult for young children. You may hear cries of "That's not fair," "It's not your turn," and "You're cheating."

Nonetheless, since children desire to be part of the social world, they will want to play rule-bound games, such as computer games, board games, and sports. This type of game playing encourages negotiation and team building.

Playing by the rules: *Geoffrey calls out: "Miss Quinton, Giles is not following the rules of the game!"*

In turn, Giles argues that Geoffrey does not understand the rules of the game.

The teacher, Lisa, then suggests that, as a group, the children define the rules. She tells them that they should work to reach a consensus on the rules and play.

Helping to sort out how to play a game and to enjoy the challenges that it may offer is part of the learning gained through rule-bound games — as in this instance, children come to see how rules can create consensus and order in how people do things. These moments allow teachers and caregivers to reinforce concepts such as fair play, patience, communication, and respect for others.

Good Games for a Classroom Games Corner

Whether a classic game or a much newer game, the games identified here will help children develop such things as a sense of fair play, an appreciation of rules, and a willingness to co-operate.

Classic Games

Connect 4	Sorry	Candy Land
Trouble	Hungry Hungry Hippo	Battleship
Operations	Scrabble Junior	Guess Who
Chinese Checkers	Hi Ho Cherry-O	Chutes and Ladders

New Games

- The Sneaky Snacky Squirrel Game helps reinforce color matching, strategic thinking, turn-taking, and motor skills.
- Blokus is a logical strategy game with simple rules. Players compete to place 21 pieces on a board touching pieces of the same color.
- Hoot Owl Hoot is a simple strategy game that encourages reading and social skills. Children help owls fly back to their nests. Everyone wins if all owls make it back before nightfall.
- Outfoxed, a co-operative detective game, involves children in figuring out who is the culprit.
- Sum Swamp encourages math skills and fluency.
- Race to the Treasure, a team-based game, calls on children to work together to collect three keys and beat an ogre to a treasure.
- Sequence for Kids encourages logical thinking by lining up cards and chips in a row.

Play as Process — Digging to China

A few minutes spent observing a room full of active children easily confirms the principle that children's play worlds often show signs of their active engagement and learning. In any early childhood education program, there is almost always a buzz of energy in the room, as children move from place to place, group to group, and activity to activity. Although all that activity may appear chaotic to the onlooker, it is full of new understanding and learning on the part of the players. Knowledge use and exploration of the play world is not static; it is constantly moving and changing as children transform their knowing into something relevant and new. Children are learning all the time, turning every experience into new understanding as well as allowing us to gain new ways of thinking about the criteria that define play.

For example, play promotes positive dispositions such as curiosity, mindfulness, perseverance, determination, and helpfulness. It also encourages children to have positive dispositions towards learning in academic, intellectual, and social ways (Papatheodorou & Moyles, 2012, p. 44). According to Bertram and Pascal (2002), independence, creativity, self-motivation, and resilience are dispositions that successful learners exhibit. Such dispositions are important for learners when engaging in the process of play.

Play as process orientation

A group of children scramble onto the playground . . .
 "Let's dig a hole," says George.
 "Oh, I know, oh, I know, we can make it go somewhere," says Seth, ". . . like China."
 "Where's China?" asks a third child.
 "Well, I know . . . I know . . . that if you dig really far down you can get there. Let's use these big rocks for shovels. Let's be secret agents and go to China and . . . ," expands George.
 "Yeah, . . . we can pretend we are rescuing my little brother," says Seth, getting into the spirit of the imaginary exercise. "My mom always asks my little brother if he is digging to China."
 They grab rocks and begin to dig deep into the gravel, digging vigorously, their effort to reach China both exciting and for the moment entirely plausible to them.

This spontaneous play shows the power of imagination and possibility for learning for children. The value of this play to these small friends speaks to the possibility of their successful mission.

The dig for China lasts for three recesses, and a teacher observes how the children are progressing. Engaging in conversation with them, she deliberately asks open-ended questions:
 "How is the dig going? When do you think you will arrive there? What is the circle here?" (She points to a drawn circle in the gravel.)

The teacher's questions prompt the children to activate their imaginations but also their problem-solving skills. Back in the classroom, the teacher places relevant books about China on the reading table and points out a Chinese flag on the world map.

The children's chat reveals a great repository of knowledge. They talk about the sizes and shapes of rocks, how to hold the digging rock to get in deeper. Together, they shape the narrative frame of their mission. They discuss among themselves how far away China is, how many planes they might need to take to get there, the fact that the Olympics have been held there, and how it would take a week to reach China by boat.

The teacher observes how play can be complex and varied, as children verbally create the fantasy of the play and as the mission to China eventually becomes intermingled with a discussion of their upcoming field trip. In this symbolic play scenario, the children are motivated to accomplish their mission. Their vivid imaginations, spurred on by spontaneous play, represent both their real and imagined worlds. Children construct a meaningful place out of their environment, changing and building a scenario as new information is shared. This hands-on activity shows how they experience the play through something they can relate to — playing in a sandbox.

By the third day of the digging to China play episode, the energy for the dig has dwindled, and two of the children have wandered off to test their skills on the bars. One child remains at the dig site, working diligently to find China.

Sharing their previously acquired knowledge gave the boys an opportunity to investigate their world using all their senses, problem-solving together as they built their story narrative. In all facets, these children have learned through active engagement.

The process orientation of the play allows children to create meaning in their imagined worlds. In the above observation, we see how children's attention is really focused on the process of finding an imagined space — the end product has not necessarily consumed their interest. Although the original goal was to reach China, several times the three children abandoned that play to create their "garage," a space in the dirt to place their digging rocks, as well as straws and other small toys. They thereby shifted the play to engage in offshoots of the original narrative.

Process orientation is a shifting of understanding or learning through the play itself. The product is less important than children achieving this act of learning and developing these skills during the play. Children may be focusing on the making of a nameless product, but that does not negate the importance of what they are doing. For example, perhaps they are copying the rays of the sun from the teacher's illustration onto their own calendar or pasting the body of a snowman together. What is important is watching how scissors cut the paper or how the glue can stick things together, or beginning to understand how to represent the physical world through art. This process orientation in play is important to children's development and key to their orientation to their world. Although adults may misunderstand the process because it seems to show a lack of focus, children's easy tendency to become distracted is part and parcel of a process orientation. It is how children come to understand how things work.

Intrinsic motivation

In the digging to China play scenario, all three children were intrinsically motivated to achieve their goal, which had little to do with basic needs or the demands of their peers. Their enthusiasm shows how they worked together in the process of the playmaking. Each day the children stepped outside the classroom door and were motivated by the play.

The defining of the play in the dig to China shows many opportunities for the children's learning, as well as demonstrating how the children are intrinsically motivated to play. Motivation to play can arise from several sources. For example, the creation of imagined worlds may derive from a child's desire to be in an individual space. Left alone, children will initiate spontaneous and motivated play scenarios that bring them great joy and satisfaction and allow them to show power over their own learning and play.

Teachers need to keep in mind the importance of self-initiated play and motivated play activities. Children derive great enjoyment and satisfaction from them, despite their lack of adult input. The process of digging to China was inherently rewarding for the three children. No concrete lesson was achieved, but as pointed out above, they were learning to orient themselves within the world. Although the intrinsic aspects of the play were not obvious, this does not make them less valuable to the children's learning.

Non-literal, or free, play

Non-literal, or free, play calls for free thinking and exploration. As children engage in the narrative frames of play, they devise new possibilities and extensions for their play. New environments and problems are developed and subsequently played out as they explore *what if*. Children are often willing to suspend the world of reality, using everyday objects to suit their narrative play frame. For the young diggers, straws became shovels and small erasers, dump trucks.

The dialogic engagement between children in play can encompass both their real and imagined worlds. A teacher watching this type of play can often see how a child's home reality is represented. This type of play may demonstrate what children know, what they don't know, what they want to bring to the learning experience, and what they are trying to negotiate. The non-literal quality of play shows a child's ability to negotiate new experiences, a needed skill for life.

Experimentation with rules

Another characteristic found in play is children's great desire to experiment with rules. Play constantly alters the rules about what can and cannot happen. Children's play is in a constant state of negotiation. The rules of play and, by transference, the rules of social negotiation, are greatly dependent upon the prior knowledge and the cultural backgrounds that children bring to the play space. These rules are implicit and often cannot be articulated to adults. Young children do not like to be bound by rules and come to accept them only over time. In many of their other interactions, say, with parents, they have no control over rules and must accept them. Experimentation with the play rules provides a safe opportunity for problem solving, critical thinking, and risk taking.

During the dig to China, the children negotiated where to dig "to make a difference" and where to locate the garage for the tools. They changed the rules of the game to suit the interest of the moment. Children's experimentation with rules allows them to gain problem-solving abilities and perhaps to see into the worlds of others. During play like the dig, children easily develop mutual understandings of the forms for the play. The flexibility of their rules teaches them much useful knowledge, such as how to negotiate with the world around them.

Play as Work

Play is hard work. The mind is engaged with the construction and reconstruction of the world. Inquiry-based learning requires focus and concentrated engagement. It is in a constant state of design and redesign, in order to accommodate the suggestions of the play scenario.

As noted earlier, in a very real way, play is the work of a child. Furthermore, it is not just a way to engage children until they are ready to take on more tacit and intellectual feats, as is often suggested by books that encourage early language development in babies. Work by David Elkind (2001), as well as many others, warns that the substitution of play for instructional methodology produces what he calls "the hurried child," the child who is an anxious and dependent follower rather than a self-confident person. As we shall see, play can be a valid and useful part of the classroom experience, one that produces learning valuable to a child's self-expression, self-worth, and self-enhancement.

2

Playing with Language

When children are playing happily, they are also developing a sense of well-being. These feelings of comfort and security help them to regulate their emotions and give them opportunities to develop their interpersonal skills. Play is also an essential piece of self-regulation. *Self-regulation*, in its simplest terms, is children's ability to control their own emotions, actions, thoughts, and impulses. It is an essential part of their early years' development, and according to many researchers, it can have considerable impact on their later academic success. Games and other forms of collaborative playing are crucial for self-regulation: important concepts, such as sharing, waiting one's turn, following directions, not being too rough, and controlling frustration, are all learned on the playground and through interacting with other children. Similarly, play also encourages negotiation among children, as game rules must meet the standards and approval of all parties. Beyond self-regulation and negotiation, play is essential in developing collaboration and interaction skills; it also gives an opportunity for children to display what they have learned through observation. In turn, these skills can help children become better communicators — and good communication is the foundation of effective speaking and listening.

Inviting children to play with language will help them to think creatively. In doing so, the process by which they engage in language for problem solving and use language for varying forms of communication will become more enriched. McLeod (2018) asserts that it is important to "emphasize language learning through activities that children find familiar and meaningful. Children's language can be developed in a play setting when teachers provide the appropriate opportunities."

Literature is critical to help children be successful. When children use their imaginations and ask questions about what they read, it helps them feel that they are accomplished learners. For children to become masters of their language, they need many opportunities to test these skills, processing their creative energy through repetitive efforts.

Building a classroom environment where children can seek out different challenges and risks to become better communicators will help children develop skills essential for literacy. Not all children begin their learning in language-enriched environments, so learning how language sounds, how words are used in communication, and what the words mean is central to a balanced language arts program. Children need to be engaged and interacting with words, sounds, and language all the time for the proper development of these skills. Watching children at play shows how they can use language for their own good.

Active Engagement through Play: Piaget

Known for his theory of cognitive development, Jean Piaget talks about active engagement through play: children practise what they know and risk new experiences through testing and trying things out. As an example, when my nephew Steven was five years old, he loved to play Restaurant. He brought menus, checked our fridge for ingredients, and pretended to write a list of what we ordered, discussing which dishes he felt were the healthiest for us.

After enacting this scenario many times, Steven asked his parents if he could go to a "real restaurant with tablecloths." Bravely, his parents decided to let him do so. As soon as they had ordered their food, Steven advised the waiter that he had to check the fridge to make sure that the restaurant had the necessary ingredients. In play moments like this, children develop real-world connections between their experiences and what they explore in play; they can also learn social cues in real-life scenarios.

Lev Vygotsky reminds us that children's play worlds help to develop their thought processes. He also reminds us that proper learning and development are dependent on healthy social relationships. Social development literally is child's play in Vygotsky's eyes due to his belief that play offers children a more sophisticated array of social skills to use in problem-solving situations. This high-level engagement during playtime helps children navigate social problems and understand how to play by the rules. Vygotsky (1988, p. 191) states that "the very mechanism underlying higher mental functions is a copy from social interaction; all higher mental functions are internalised social relationships."

During recess one day, one of my students asked me to hold his "plane ticket" (a field-trip permission slip with a suitable airline symbol pasted on the folded paper). He announced he was going to Florida for the winter break and would be leaving with many of his classmates at playtime after lunch. Other children became interested in the game, and as I listened, I could hear familiar airport codes and an announcer saying, "Plane 424 leaving now for Florida — bring your ticket." Children arrived with their own versions of tickets. The air was filled with commands to "buckle up" and "show your passport here." Playing Airport for these children was a lead-in to discussions about travel, holidays, and family times, but, most important, it contributed to their language development: they gained practical understanding of the vocabulary of travel and location.

Oral Language Development as Part of Emergent Literacy

Often overlooked in the race to teach young children to read is the development of their oral language abilities and their role in good communication. The progression of child language development is correlated with the development of facial, tongue, and dental growth. Many children struggle with oral language, and strategies that involve play often prove helpful. By way of definition, when we speak of *oral language*, we are referring to abilities that involve children's skills at speaking and listening. More specifically, we are referring to children's ability to acquire vocabulary and language, their phonological awareness, their knowledge of letters and words, their comprehension of meaning, and their ability to follow storytelling, read-alouds, and other narratives.

When children come to school, and during their first years, they are still very much in emergent literacy, constructing their understanding of language, how it works, and how it is relevant to their needs and lives. Over time, they understand that language and its use is critical to their being able to engage with others socially. They learn that language serves a purpose and is used in differing contexts, and that understanding these differing contexts will be beneficial to them.

Researchers William Teale and Elizabeth Sulzby (1986) studied children's emergent literacy for some time and reached several conclusions about how it works. Their ideas serve as simple guidelines for us as educators when we begin to assist children in attaining oral language development.

1. Literacy develops when children interact with reading, writing, and oral language in their homes and communities. That is where they learn what language is, how to use it, and what purposes it can serve.
2. Children's literacies begin to emerge long before they enter school. Within their families and communities, they acquire many skills.

3. These home- and family-based experiences contribute to later formal literacy education and are crucial to children's overall language development.
4. Interactions with adults are crucial in laying the foundations for children's language and literacy development.
5. All children learn and acquire language at different rates and move through stages at different speeds.

Although "school literacy" has often been rather narrowly perceived as only reading and writing, early learning for young children is multimodal; in other words, children use many different text forms to engage in literacy acts (Kress, 2005). These acts include speaking, gesturing, aural communication, and other forms of personal expression, such as drawing. The process by which children use these language forms is developmental. It begins at birth, continues throughout childhood, and carries on into adulthood. The playmaking in the early years of children's lives, however, fulfills a formal role in their ability to communicate. Children experience literacy within environmental and social contexts that help them make sense of how their reading and writing fit within their own social world and the one around them. As emerging readers and writers, children want to make sense of what they read and write. They benefit when they can use these skills in meaningful activities that require active participation. In the example below, Laura Huckle used a community event to encourage an elaborate play activity, which, in turn, required considerable use of communication skills.

Laura, teaching in a Grade 1 classroom in St. John, New Brunswick, was striving to situate the children's reading and writing within their local community. To encourage children to build their oral skills, she began a discussion about the farmers' market. She brought in newspaper clippings, discussing the idea of a market, and asked the children to help make a list of the jobs at the market. Children engaged in small-group discussions about the jobs, having conversations such as the following.

    Henry: *When my grand-dad took me to the market last week . . . I mean Saturday . . . um . . . we bought hot chocolate and waffles. . . . I know that could be a job. Someone sells hot chocolate and waffles.*

    Madison: *Yeah . . . Yeah . . . I got hot chocolate, too. You know what . . . you know what? I think that when we went, we got eggs. Yeah, we did.*

    George: *You know what you were saying (gesturing to Madison), we could have someone to take the . . . take the money. Yeah, that would be good.*

    This discussion encouraged the children to use their oral and communication skills to share what they already knew about jobs at the market. Laura drew on their discussions, asking each group to share one idea. The discussion included all the children and provided a mutual understanding of the local market. Laura bridged this knowledge to a writing and representation activity.

    Children made multimodal representations of what they knew to share with others. They worked in small groups, drawing pictures in comic-strip form of what each person would do at a market. They thereby shared their literacy experiences in a way that evolved from their social and environmental contexts.

    Laura also used their understanding of what it meant to communicate within a group. Some children drew a road map of how to get to the market, showing various familiar stores and restaurant signs, such as McDonald's, and a nearby fire station. Another group drew and cut out pictures of vegetables that would be sold and discussed colors of vegetables and tastes according to color. One boy reported he felt that green vegetables should not be eaten, while another child argued strongly about the virtues of a balanced diet. Later on, one group of the children used puppet role-playing about shopping at the market, furthering their oral skills in playmaking.

Students in one group discussed the colors and tastes of vegetables at the market after drawing pictures of common ones.

This vignette shows us how children engage in many different language processes to inform themselves of the world around them. The processes of oral language call upon all the social and cognitive ways in which children come to literacy. Meaning is gained from active participation, where children construct social understanding — in this case, of the market — as well as from their skills and knowledge, shared in their oral language and play-based activities. Based on this vignette, we can confirm the importance of the knowledge that children bring to the classroom.

Literacy is socially constructed, and, in this example, we see how the children develop it in the context of the market. They interact with one another, adopting different forms, such as speaking and listening, problem solving through discussion, writing, role-playing, and drawing, and we gain insight into the rich literacy context that forms the basis of the children's knowledge. These children share "funds of knowledge," which Moll, Amanti, Neff, and Gonzales (1992) defined as the ways in which we all form understanding of our experiences. Meaningful role play boosts learning potential for language development, problem solving, and mathematical cognition. Ultimately, we must consider oral language as a part of everyday living that is socially and culturally situated (Barton & Hamilton, 2000). Embracing the valuable learning and oral language experiences that define children's first literacy engagements with the world is needed for later success (Heath, 1983). Teachers who see the value of embedding oral language in how children view the world and within their individual contexts strengthen the foundations of literacy that children have when they come to school.

On the next page is a line master that can be shared with the parents of the students in your class.

Phonics in the Home

Authentic teaching moments at home, in child-care centres, and in early years' classrooms help children to feel comfortable exploring and experimenting with language. Here are some playful ways to engage children in exploring sounds and letters.

- Bring words and sounds into your conversation. For example, if you see a train, talk about the sounds it makes: "The train goes choo-choo; you need to put a *c* and an *h* together to make that sound."

- Once in a while, read aloud books that use a lot of alliteration, such as Janet and Allan Ahlberg's *Each Peach Pear Plum* or Jeffie Ross Gordon's *Six Sleepy Sheep*. Encourage your child to speak the words with you after a few readings. Once you feel that your child is ready, invite him or her to sound out words based on the first letter.

- Read alphabet books or make one together by drawing fancy letters or cutting out letters from print advertisements and catalogues.

- Make up flashcards that show simple sound units, such as short /u/ or /b/ — these are called "phonemes." Ask your child to say them aloud.

- Point out letters, and their sounds, in your environment: "Look. That sign says 'STOP.' Can you make that sound?"

- Play letter-based scavenger and treasure hunts: "Can you find a word for something in the room that has the /oo/ sound?"

- Place plastic magnetic letters on the fridge, and perhaps during meal preparation times, play this game: "Can you find the letters to make a /b/ sound? a /th/ sound?" Alphabet blocks can serve the same function.

- Share tongue twisters. The tongue twisters help children appreciate the differences between sounds, while providing amusement. Children love to recite these together, perhaps competing playfully to see who can say them without errors. *She sells seashells at the seashore* is a great example, but there are many others, including these.

A big bug bit the little beetle, but the little beetle bit the big bug back.
The black bug bled black blood.
Betty bought butter but the butter was bitter, so Betty bought better butter to make the bitter butter better.
How much wood could a woodchuck chuck if a woodchuck could chuck wood?
I scream. You scream. We all scream for ice cream!

And the one that even parents and teachers struggle with:
Irish wristwatch . . . Irish wristwatch

Pembroke Publishers © 2019 *Invitations to Play* by Anne Burke. ISBN 978-1-55138-336-1

Sounds and Letters — Making the Links

Most children can speak quite clearly long before they can read. Many will have some grasp of the links between sounds and letters via constant recitation of the ABCs. Discovering that letters can have more than one sound or be combined to create more sounds can be difficult to grasp. Although that is just one part of the puzzle, it is one necessary to successful reading and writing.

As stated earlier, the best way to ensure that a child successfully navigates the shoals of emergent literacy is through the provision of a stimulating home life and community, full of play and opportunities for language use. Consider, though, that most parents will have only a vague recollection of the term *phonics*, one area in which their children will need help. As we know, phonics essentially describes the relationship between the sounds of language and the written letters, or combinations of letters. These sounds are called "phonemes."

When introducing phonics concepts, adults will find it valuable to remember that children need to hear language in a familiar and meaningful context. Emphasizing the sounds of words as opposed to just saying the words and the letters will greatly help children in their efforts to become readers. Be sure to remind parents that this should be a logical extension of their current playful conversation and coaching, rather than any obvious effort.

Exploring phonemes

Phonemes, the sounds that make up the auditory form of the English language, are represented by letters and groups of letters. Although many phonemes use just one letter, some use two or three. In most standard North American English dialects, there are about 40 sounds but only 26 letters to represent them. Various combinations of letters are required to create the rest of the sounds, /ch/ and /th/ being two examples. Some groups of different letters can be used to make the same sound, too. For example, the hard /a/ of "bake" and the /a/ sound in "gain" are made by different letters. Spelling is not necessarily a good guide for phonemes; for example, the hard /e/ sound can be made several ways (e.g., **fe**et and b**ea**t).

Although there are six vowels — a, e, i, o, u, and y — there are 10 distinct vowel sounds used in English, not all of which correspond to their originating vowel. These include the short /e/ (beg), long /e/ (beet), short /a/ (bat), long /a/ (fate), short /o/ (blog), long /o/ (blow), short /i/ (fit), long /i/ (fight, my), short /u/ (luck), long /u/ (duke), and other vowel-based sounds, such as /oi/ (toy), /oo/ (fool), and /ear/ (gear). Keep in mind that if a child has been exposed to other languages, he or she may have knowledge of even more sounds. French and Spanish, for example, are quite common in North America, and both contain vowel sounds that differ widely from those used in English.

Consonant phonemes are a bit easier, often corresponding more specifically to the alphabet sounds a child may already know. Phonemes made from combined letters — such as *ch* (chair), *sh* (shop), and *th* (this) — will take longer to get established.

Early Understandings about Talk

At an early age, children develop their understanding of how language works. Indeed, infants can determine differences between various languages, displaying a preference for the language their mother uses. All babies make similar sounds in their first months of life no matter the language spoken around them. All babies have the capability to produce the sounds used in every known language. This finding about how children learn to speak is interesting because it means that in the first few years of life, every baby is capable of learning how to speak and comprehend every human language.

Parents are amazed at how quickly children discover that language serves different purposes depending on the ways and context of use. Children learn through language — what and how it is used — to communicate with others. In their early language use, children draw on a wide range of vocabulary and expressions that vary according to whom they are talking.

Young children develop many understandings about talk. For example, they come to realize that the way we use our voices varies according to the context: quiet voices for the library and outside voices for the playground. Children also quickly understand that choice of words spoken is influenced by the circumstances. On a basic level, toddlers and babies are guided to listen to the sounds of spoken language. Over time, children discover that all language serves a purpose. Therefore, we must ensure that talk is purposeful and planned so that young children learn the appropriate places and contexts for its use.

To become good communicators, children need certain skills that can be both taught and practised. Taking turns when sharing ideas, negotiating differences in opinions, and learning how to share information individually as well as in a group are important beginning steps for children. Giving children the opportunity to both talk and listen to one another is crucial in early years' settings. Sharing and explaining their thoughts and opinions builds confidence within the children.

Planning for Meaningful Talk

Children learn through meaningful engaged interactions whereby they share in the literacy event. When children see the benefit of talking — to share and explore their ideas — they become engaged in developing their own literacy.

It is valuable to encourage young children to use language in a purposeful manner. Doing so will enable them to share ideas in collaborative settings. It will also help them cope with the conflicts that are sure to arise in an early years' setting. Inexperienced with conflict, children need opportunities to explore ways to resolve problems through playmaking. Helping children find the appropriate forms of language and the ways in which to express their feelings acceptably prepares them for more formal schooling tasks. Regulation of their emotions happens when they feel that they are competent communicators. Children have a strong sense of injustice and can feel isolated if they have been wronged in some way.

Learning to read children's non-verbal expressions, such as their facial expressions, gestures, and posture, helps educators understand the children's needs. The larger numbers of children coming to school with delayed speech abilities also require educators to pay more attention to children's non-verbal communication (Canadian Language and Literacy Research Network, 2009; Miller & Almon,

Communicating through Charades
Trevor Mackenzie, the teacher of a large, diverse class of Grade 1 students, found a good way to draw out some of the class's more reluctant communicators: Charades. He simplified the game and the rules, so that one child acted out a household task, while three other children with varying skills guessed what the task was.

"I asked them to explain what the actor was doing," said Trevor. "The key thing was that the children were so focused on what the actor was doing, they didn't worry about how they were saying it. The game also really appealed to their sense of humor — they loved to play it, even the students with little English."

2009). Understanding the meanings that children associate with these physical forms of communication will help us to communicate with them and to build on their language skills. Although we may not always be aware of our actions as teachers, we need to be sensitive to the non-verbal messages that children can easily pick up on.

Helping Children Communicate

- Model good listening for the children. Hold eye contact as they talk to you. For children who are more physically active, hold a hand to show that you are still listening, even if they find it difficult to keep eye contact.
- Observe and respectfully acknowledge the importance of the messages that children communicate to you. Ask yourself questions like these: Do I understand the message? What did the child want me to say? Is there something else they wanted to share?
- Help children develop an emotional vocabulary. For example, ask: "Did that make you happy?" "Why are you mad?"
- If children find it hard to talk, lend them your voice. Guide their conversations through bridging. Model how they might talk about what they are learning. "Did you mean this, Meena?" (Repeat and offer more explanation.) "Tell me again."
- Use positive language to reinforce ideal behavior with others. "You are a good friend, Jenna, to help Henry with the blocks. I liked how you explained what we were doing. It is so important that we understand one another."

We want children to actively engage in authentic talk in creative ways that encourage them to use their imaginations. To become active participants in the classroom's circle of conversation, children need to see the use of questioning. Developing a classroom that invites creative thinking in the form of questions will inspire listening and speaking. Educators must hypothesize, imagine, wonder, project, and otherwise see the possibilities for positive conversation around them. Doing this builds a classroom with meaningful talk.

To place this idea in a classroom setting, remember that almost all children are inspired by and curious about topics that grab their interest. They are motivated to find out more about these topics. Children also intuitively understand that certain topics locate them in social and cultural contexts, and that these identities are closely linked to the talk they choose to pursue.

For example, since the age of seven, my own son has enjoyed chatting about video games, especially about how to get to the coveted "next level." He and his friends have always associated video games with being mature and skilled. Particularly when he was younger, I made a point of asking as many questions as possible — not so much because I was curious but because I wanted to encourage him to use his verbal skills to discuss and explain the topic. By showing a sincere interest in what my son likes to discuss, asking leading questions, and then following his lead, I helped him in his acquisition of language.

Developing Speech Confidence

- To help students develop the confidence to speak, strive to make a safe and secure classroom, where children feel that their opinions are valued.
- Draw out children's discussion by adding to what they have said. For example, if Gemma shows you her new rubber boots, share and build a discussion. "I like your new boots. They are red and blue. Wow! Look at the red stripes on the side! Do you like walking through puddles?" Let children hear you use descriptive language in a context that they understand. Remember, children naturally absorb language and make it their own.
- Try to extend a conversation by making a connection to the child's experiences. If John tells you that he is going to visit his grandmother, ask him what he will do at his grandmother's home. Keeping the conversation going lets the children know you are interested in them. It teaches children that communication requires attention and concentration — it is a two-way process.
- Offer access to games and activities that give many opportunities for chat, listening, and discussion.
- Provide an environment that celebrates all cultural groups and that encourages language representation from the entire group.

Drawing on the senses

Children always learn better when there is a sensory component to the play and learning scenario. With the basic games outlined below, a teacher can use children's natural sensory curiosity to enhance their speech and oral expressiveness; at the same time, children can create authentic connections with their real-world environments.

- Children love to collect things from nature. Go on a nature walk and collect stones, leaves, shells, bird feathers, tree bark, flowers, berries, and nuts. Ask children to touch these and use sensory language to describe how they feel. Ask them, too, to describe the shapes of things, their sizes, and whether they can compare them to other familiar objects.
- Play children different sounds from recordings (easily sourced on the Internet). Encourage them to identify their sources and then add information: "Do you think the dog was big or small?" "Does that person sound happy or sad?"
- Create a simple sensory scavenger hunt, which requires children to identify colors, objects, or textures around them.
- Prompt children to talk about the differences in how things taste — for example, between green and black grapes, or red and green peppers. (You might also discuss how people are the same and different — a healthy thing to do and a way to respect what makes us unique.)

Building Classroom Listening Skills

- Show and Share promotes speaking and listening. Children can bring objects to class and talk about them — a good way for English language learners to share their culture. Challenged or shy learners can show a picture or have a puppet describe their object.

- Use story bags, each containing a good-quality storybook with materials that help to support the story. Support materials may include puppets, soft toys, games, or related objects. An informational text related to any part of the narrative may be included. Sometimes, a CD or audiobook can be played to help children follow the story.

- Puppet theatres and puppets allow young children to overcome inhibitions and use their own voices to structure a narrative. The use of puppets encourages dialogue and discussion with shy students.

- Action songs and nursery rhymes help children bring actions and music together; they also help them develop a greater awareness of rhyme. Toddlers are stimulated by the sounds of rhyme and proceed to vocalize with these sounds. When children recognize rhyming in sounds and words, it facilitates their auditory discrimination. Nursery rhymes not only encourage younger children to vocalize, but also support older children in perfecting their speech sounds. Exposure to music gives rise to a plethora of questions, providing children with learning opportunities to recite aloud words, such as *beat*, *measure*, *soft*, *loud*, and *sharp*.

- Role play allows for children to try on different roles and personas. These play scenarios need not be fantastical. Children love to play in imaginary spaces that reflect the neighborhoods where they live, such as a pretend café or grocery store.

- A listening area with pre-recorded stories is helpful to children.

- Having children work in pairs encourages them to verbalize and clarify their thoughts before group discussion. It also encourages good listening and social skills.

- You can ask children to organize themselves in a straight line according to a specific criterion, such as shoe size, height, or colors.

- Soundscapes provide a good way for children to develop discerning listening skills. Via the Internet, you can easily find soundscapes, such as a park filled with children or a busy street. Once you share one with the class, prompt the students as a group to identify what they heard, and record their findings. Children can also create remembered sounds, such as those of a windstorm or rainstorm, using hand-made instruments.

Sharing their learning

Children love to share what is important to them. Teachers who invite students to share their successes and news in the classroom are, in fact, allowing them to talk about their literacy engagements. Sometimes, children informally share what they have learned at a literacy-related play centre. In this case, they are expected to account for what they have learned and set goals. Teachers then have a chance to clarify and extend some of the learning they have observed.

Narrative retelling, where a teacher asks a child to describe in more detail the topic of interest, is also important. It can scaffold greater vocabulary. Ideally, the child will retell a story in his or her own words.

Experiencing read-alouds

In terms of language and literacy development, read-alouds are among the most significant experiences children can have. The read-aloud is a way for children to increase their listening comprehension. We know from research that when they listen to literature throughout the day, children uncover new meanings and learn to make insightful connections to their own lives (Galda, Ash, & Cullinan, 2000). Read-alouds make the experience with text multi-sensory, which helps children improve their comprehension and their connection with the text. With help from the teacher, they can make connections to the world around them.

Reading aloud is a sharing of language. Hearing the language of stories and informational texts exposes children to written language structures and more complex vocabulary and difficult concepts than they would hear in normal conversation. When the teacher reads aloud from all genres of children's literature, it is a way to appeal to many different tastes. Watching the choices children make in their library selections confirms this.

The read-aloud allows the teacher to encourage oral language. Texts read to children provide alternative linguistic models that are not represented in speech. It is not enough to simply hear or read to understand new and interesting language coding; students must talk about what they have read, defend their interpretations, and explain what they have observed about the stories and the language used to tell them. Through these formative discussions, children consolidate the learning of new information.

Making a Big Book

Because of their larger size, Big Books are easy to read in front of a class. Bigger pictures and words interest students, and no one is disadvantaged because of distance. The format is easy to see, so students can make observations and recognize words with ease.

Beyond reading a Big Book, you and your class can make a Big Book. Doing so is easy. Just follow these steps:

1. Choose a story either well known or created by the group.
2. Copy each page of text onto blank sheets of paper: 25 by 15 inches is a good size.
3. Write big enough for all students in the classroom to see. Once you have finished the writing, reread the story to the class and brainstorm ideas for possible illustrations.
4. Use different mediums to illustrate the text. If students are illustrating, model or assist with their representations.
5. Help the class determine the correct page order by displaying the pages on the chalkboard, pinned around the classroom, or spread out on the floor.
6. To add a personal connection, you could create a title page featuring a class picture and noting the class name as the publishing company.

Expanding on the potential of read-alouds

To help younger students develop reading, listening, and writing skills, reading aloud should be a part of every early years' classroom; however, teachers can expand the communication and language development potential of read-alouds by adopting a few simple practices. Give a brief introduction to the book and explain why you chose it. Show the cover illustration and title; ask the students what they think the book may be about. Respond to any questions that arise as you read or build on students' ideas and understandings. Once in a while, stop and ask students what they think will happen next: "Do you think Goldilocks should try the porridge?" Be sure to ask open-ended questions with multiple possible answers, for example, "What would you have done?" Share what parts you liked best and invite the students to do the same.

Read-alouds can be extended in many other ways. They permit the teacher to scaffold the children's discussion, thereby encouraging children to make more connections. Dramatic play based on part of the story is an interactive engagement with story. After a read-aloud, the teacher may suggest that children respond at the Writing Centre through writing and drawing (see Chapter 3). Symbolic representation of characters through cut-outs enables children to share connections from their own lives.

Exploring the Nature of Story

Storytelling involves communication between a storyteller and listeners. Children who actively listen to stories grow their vocabularies, anticipate plot lines and language patterns, and predict new words or phrases, which, in turn, encourages them to experiment with language. Storytelling also creates empathy between the listeners and the storyteller, as active listeners can draw personal connections between themselves and the characters in the story.

Storytelling is very much a performance. Creating the environment for children to listen to and experience a story requires teachers to develop a persona that is both inviting and engaging. Teachers who tell their students stories must make sure that all students are engaged and actively listening. Choosing a story of the appropriate level and using gestures, different voices, volume changes, and pacing (variations in delivery speed) will do much to hold students' interest.

Expressing understanding of a story

In her Senior Kindergarten classroom, Leslie reads aloud *The Paper Bag Princess* by Robert Munsch to her young students. Through this story, students are introduced to many forms of language. They engage in both reading and a critical sharing of viewpoints; through her questioning, Leslie helps the children to understand both the narrative form of story and some relevant themes.

After an animated reading of the book, about a girl who defies gender stereotypes to become a princess on her own terms, Leslie engages her class in a discussion of friendship, stereotypes, and gender.

Leslie: What did you like about the story? Kieran?

Kieran: Well, I liked the end. I think that Ronald is a bad friend . . . a bad prince.

Leslie: You do? Why is he not a good friend? Why do you think that?

Kieran: Because even when Elizabeth saved him from the dragon, he did not say thank-you. He told her to change her dirty clothes because she did not look like a princess.

Daneisha: (interjecting) . . . yeah, that, and also, too, that he thinks that she should wear princess clothes.

Leslie: Do you think princesses should always dress a certain way?

Daneisha: They wear pink, I know *(listening to others talking about what princesses should wear)* . . . but, you know, she saved him from the dragon and got her clothes burned for him. He is a bum. *(repeating the last line of the book)*

Leslie: And so, he is not a good friend?

Seth: No, not a good friend. He just wants everyone to be the way he wants.

The children express their understanding through play at classroom play centres. At the Writing and Drawing Centre, children re-create the story in a collaborative setting, as they determine which parts of the story need to be illustrated and shared.

These images were inspired by a reading and discussion of The Paper Bag Princess.

The children also re-create and re-enact the main points of the story using costumes, while others work on building the castle in the blocks area. Other children repeat parts of the story using the puppets in the dramatic play area. The classroom is alive as the children create and re-create the story narrative, honing oral language skills.

Fairy tales as teaching tools

Children's creativity must be expanded by a high level of support for their curiosity, play, and exploration. Whether traditional or modern, fairy tales as a literary genre cultivate imaginative thought processes and offer a way for children to come to terms with their individual thoughts, feelings, and ideas about the stories. There is a plethora of fairy tales, all useful in teaching children about character, story structure, and setting. Fairy tales provide the option for children to add to them, create alternative endings, and fabricate new characters. To invite children to experiment with the aspects of a fairy tale is to bestow on them an opportunity to gain key reading and writing skills.

Oftentimes, these tales have a central focus on certain values, morals, and lessons — values that might be much at odds with what the children have been taught. Discussion and activities about these life lessons encourage personal growth. When children relate to a character's qualities such as bravery and kindness, they are not only developing a better understanding of plot, motivation, conflict, and characterization but also the important understanding of what it means to have an informed opinion.

Stories as identity

Stories are a part of all of us. They are a vital way in which we learn about ourselves and the nature of the world around us. Watch story time at a library sometime. Even without the visual excitement of a screen, children intently listen to and look at the story, conveyed through the expression in the speaker's voice paired with the picture book's illustrations.

Oral storytelling requires children to exercise concentration and memory if they are to grasp what the story is about. Well read or told, a good story will capture children's sense of wonder, confirm what they know and understand, and expand upon their interests and curiosity. Listening to stories about other children and other parts of the world will require them to share the viewpoints and emotions of others. Through the shared listening experience, children can also learn to appreciate the different opinions and viewpoints that they may be exposed to. According to professional storyteller Marie L. Shedlock (1951), storytelling is important because it allows students to imagine, wonder, develop a sense of humor, learn about how actions have consequences, and interpret ideals.

Exploring narrative structure

In creating a classroom where children and their viewpoints are accepted, we want our choice of literature to provide new learning, but also to help children understand the patterns and sequences by which we make sense of our world. Whether this is through a book about the passage of the seasons or a Robert Munsch story used to make a moral point, the narrative structure, or an organizational map for this learning, is a necessary element of the early-grade classroom. Through the critical thought process that comes with storytelling and subsequent discussions, children come to understand new vocabulary, and how (and when) it may have different meanings. By an interconnecting of the written text and picture book illustrations, students also come to understand that the two aspects work together to create meaning in the narrative structure. This insight assists them in oral language when they are retelling the story to others.

In Leslie's classroom, children used their expressive language and became part of a critical discussion about how the protagonist stands up for herself — they questioned stereotypical viewpoints on dress and image. Through their play, they developed their oral language and shared their critical understanding of *The Paper Bag Princess*. In Leslie's play-based classroom, other activities, such as puppet play, allowed children to explore what it means to judge people by their clothes. The students decided that Prince Ronald was "just behaving badly." Building upon this response, Leslie asked them to retell the story using the puppets. As they did so through their play, children shared the voices of the characters as well as catch phrases from the picture book. Their comprehension was empowered.

Verbal retelling of the story showed the children's understanding of a complex theme, such as identity. Their addition of a scene — one where the prince apologizes to the princess — showed how they explored the varying ideas within the plot and extended original ideas. In this case, the children's small-group discussions led to explorations of the themes. Collaborative play through painting, drawing, puppet acting, and role play using a blocks area to create the castle setting enabled the children to feel and live the story; it reinforced the narrative structure and allowed them to use their own words and draw on their own cultural understandings. The imaginative play that ensued throughout the day developed the children's oral language, some of which was quite complex. Children shared differing viewpoints on the characters, perspectives, and ways to address acceptance and difference.

Puppetry in storytelling

Whether as audience or as presenters, most children are entertained by puppets. Puppets can represent people or objects in real-life scenarios or help children imagine through play. Children can also use puppets as the characters of a story that they are told. Puppets help children focus on tasks and stories that can assist them in gathering new information. Through children's imaginative play, puppets can also help students practise problem-solving skills, critical thinking skills, and critical listening skills. If students are manipulating puppets in groups, working towards a common narrative conclusion, the shared use of the puppets encourages co-operation, communication, and self-awareness. Finally, puppets encourage personal expression, perhaps freeing children to vocalize anxiety or develop creative thinking.

Play scenarios to extend storytelling

Once a story is told (or read), children can draw on their imaginations to engage in many play scenarios. Using these forms helps children play out stories for further character exploration and understanding of narrative forms. The following recommendations offer specific ways in which an educator can expand upon the themes and ideas of a story, using play scenarios.

- Make use of storyboards. Ask children critical questions about the characters to show how the characters could change their situations.
- The use of puppets lets children express the characters' voices and the viewpoints that they may have about the narrative retelling.
- Give children musical instruments to play at the appearance of a character or for a scene change to help them understand story framing and sequencing.
- Let children explore how music can create an appropriate mood for the action in the story — happy, sad, even spooky. Associating music with certain contexts and settings can encourage imaginative thought.
- From a story bag, pass children objects that are noted in the story. Children then continue a retelling of the story with their own voices, which builds confidence with storytelling and narrative frame understanding.
- Using pictures and photographs contributes to the imaginative creation of the story. By way of example, a teacher could follow up an animal story by holding a picture of a dog and saying, "This is a picture of my dog and he is . . ."

The sharing of home life stories

Teachers can also use the stories of children's lives to promote oral communication. In the vignette that follows, a Grade 2 teacher shows how events outside the school may be honored and given a place in developing children's oral skills.

Teacher Kelly Ellis makes time to honor the home literacy events of her students. She believes that parents hold an important key to their children coming to understand stories. In her Grade 2 class, each student is asked to share a scrapbook of a special family event. Adam, an English language learner, shared his trip to the zoo to see polar bears. When he spoke to the class about his trip, Kelly assisted him through prompting and putting the event in a narrative form. Adam wrote and illustrated the event, and then talked to the class about his zoo experience.

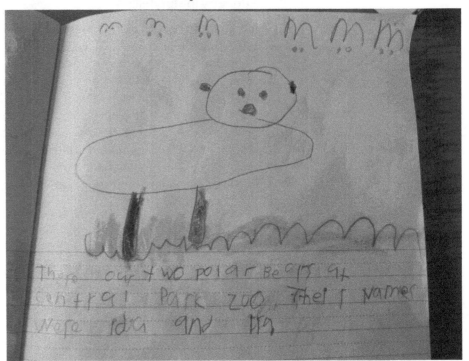

The student who saw polar bears in Central Park Zoo talked to the class about the experience after illustrating and writing about the event.

Getting Children Ready to Listen

For many of the children you teach, storytelling and read-alouds, and the listening skills that go with them, will have occurred only at bedtime. Listening skills, which all children need to develop, take practice. Before you begin reading aloud a story in the classroom, suggest that children adopt a "listening formation," such as legs crossed, with hands in laps and eyes focused on you. This enables children to equate certain actions with key words. Keep in mind that many children who have been read to at home are likely used to listening lying down. This practice is fine, too, if the classroom space allows it. Whether they are sitting or lying, their comfort level will determine how attentive they are.

Creating a space for story sharing

Space can be an issue. In many of the classes I have visited, I have noticed that neither the outdoor physical space nor the classroom space permits the creation of quiet or comfortable listening places. Some early years' teachers use a quilt or a piece of material to indicate where the story will be shared.

Effective teachers draw upon the imaginative abilities of children when engaging them in storytelling. When I spent time observing primary teachers in London, England, I found that even though their school structure varies from those in North America, they used similar strategies for storytelling. For example, in her early years' classroom in inner-city London, Karen Norman invites children to imagine that they are journeying by rocket ship to the planet Imagination. She prompts children to think of themselves as being in a space where all stories can become real and true. "Now let's pretend that we have just landed on our special place. Find a space where you are comfortable — imagine that you are there." Here, the invitation for the story session makes it more intimate for the children. Children are listening and focused. When the time comes, they want to engage in creative playmaking.

Teaching listening

Teaching listening skills to children requires much time, attention, and patience. If a student does not practise listening skills at home, teachers must work to close these learning gaps. Teaching listening consumes much instructional effort in early years' classrooms. Educators employ a variety of methods, such as repetition, to accommodate these learners at school. Many parents also instinctively use techniques to encourage literacy through listening at home. These techniques include the following:

- *Pointing out:* Talk about why listening is important. Ask questions or give instructions, and then summarize the answers the child gives.
- *Providing an example:* Illustrate the behavior you want the child to learn and the child will copy it.
- *Making suggestions:* Offering hints can help children listen and understand. Guide the child towards an appropriate response by giving suggestions, asking questions, or prompting the child to copy the expected behavior.
- *Mimicking:* Encourage children to repeat special rhymes, listening for the nuances and rhythmic tricks.
- *Giving back:* Noting an appropriate response involves offering praise and encouragement as well as highlighting exactly what you wanted the child to do.

Building Story Skills

Story skills can be developed and enhanced using any number of educational resources, from wordless picture books to simple finger puppets.

Use wordless picture books to teach children how to read and understand illustrations.

Children marvel at the opportunity to provide the text to accompany the visuals in wordless books. It is a great way for them to develop their oral language and written skills. Since all wordless books draw upon the creative imagination of the reader, this type of book appeals to young and older children alike. Wordless books may be shared to show the sequencing of a plot. Children can talk about what they may already know from the illustrations and can be encouraged to share other understandings of the narrative. Guiding the children with "thinking" questions can be helpful: "What is happening in this picture? How do you know?" "What do you think comes next? And why is that?" The rich detail offered in wordless books invites children to share other memories or experiences they may have had. Focusing the children's attention on the visual allows them to develop their observation skills, which are needed for our increasingly visual world.

Use sounds and music to build the story frame.

In building the children's auditory skills, the use of simple sound effects to create the settings for stories and develop the events can be very enjoyable. Being able to recognize particular sounds — for example, a doorbell, the wind, or animals — helps children to identify vocabulary that can be used for building transitions within a story. A story that builds on repetition can reinforce vocabulary and transitions within the story. In "The Three Billy Goats Gruff," for instance, you can ask the children what kind of sound the smallest goat would make as he crosses the bridge. Invite the children to create sounds through easily available objects, such as rice or pebbles in containers, using spoons to make the clip-clop sound, or even just clapping their hands. This activity leads young children to examine their own hand motions. Another story that explores language and can use musical instruments is Michael Rosen's popular *We're Going on a Bear Hunt*.

Use finger puppets to help tell the story.

Developing a story's plot line through use of character finger puppets helps children understand the basics of storytelling. Use of the puppets adds more dimension to the storytelling session. Through movement children actively engage in the session. Providing gestural movement for a puppet adds to the fun. Creating a voice and making choices using the puppet's gestural actions all contribute to the story's retelling. Children's vocabulary is strengthened by their association of words with actions. Playmaking with puppets makes the storytelling more experiential and will aid the children in remembering details in the plot, which is helpful with the retelling of traditional tales. The puppets can be as simple as character pictures from comic books, catalogues, or even computer-generated illustrations, all cut out and attached to craft sticks. Basic illustrations, such as the sun, clouds, a forest, or a house, will help dramatize the story setting in an active playmaking session.

Showing understanding through storytelling

We teach children about story structures and the importance of language, in part, because we hope that they will eventually be able to share their own experiences of learning. Telling a story is their way of interpreting and showing understanding of what they know. For children to become effective speakers, we first need to pique their interest in expressing ideas and narratives they know something about. Asking children to share aloud from their own cultural traditions and family stories will help them appreciate the value of oral traditions. When we build an oral storytelling culture with children, we can expect them to value hearing stories shared through speech.

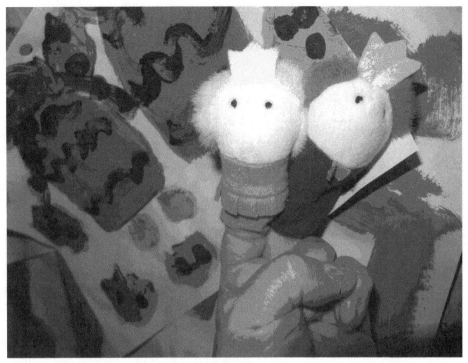

These simple puppets establish character gender and royal blood. The child art helps create the setting for storytelling.

Asking Questions about Story Play

Children often portray a story through improvised play that allows them to explore the many possibilities of story. Asking questions will help build their oral language skills and how they can bring new information to their version of the story. For example, the Kindergarten teacher named Leslie asked these questions of children after reading an exciting fantasy story.

Leslie: Tell me, Liam, why is the dragon sleeping?

Liam: Because . . . because he is pooped after doing all of that flying around the room.

Leslie: What do you think he should do when he wakes up?

Kate: He should say he is sorry to the princess.

Leslie: How might he do that?

Using key questions such as *who*, *what*, *where*, *when*, and *why* will help children generate more details from the plot. This creative thought process, stimulated by asking many kinds of questions as a part of the story-making session, helps children learn that story is built on many imaginative possibilities. Improvising scenes of what could happen beyond the plot will prompt children to use their imaginations and creativity. Your questions during play in a story structure activity will help children to share what they know about the story and to expand upon these ideas through improvisation.

Playing Story Characters

Playmaking drama can enhance children's understanding of the text. Children who act out stories develop vocabulary and use more complex language. The retelling of a story can be performed in the children's own language. Children can work together to develop a loose script. Within reason, the children should decide upon their own characters, and which characters speak which lines. Children can even take a copy of the script home to share with their families. If the "script" gets performed, the children should be listed as its authors.

Students can become the characters in a story, taking roles and improvising how to play them. Playful drama encourages students to explore stories, characters, motivations, opinions, and issues that can have an impact on their learning and creativity: it forces students to work with subject material in a new and interesting way. To develop a script and story, students must consider multiple perspectives, have confidence in their interpretation, justify decisions, think and reason, and be imaginative. Students will portray a character using information gleaned from the story but will also use components and experiences from their own lives to construct the narratives. Ultimately, the teacher is given insight into their lives.

Students can play the characters themselves or use puppets. When children engage in this kind of play, they will assume different characters and determine what they will say. Young children already have a sense of coding and language patterns; they will voice the roles of adults and children differently, for example. They will also use their own ideas for the order of appearance of the characters and settings.

Some ways that students can use character-based dramatic play are as follows.

Character on the Hot Seat: A student takes on the role of a character and sits on a chair in front of the class. Perhaps the student has chosen to become Goldilocks from "Goldilocks and the Three Bears." Students from the class ask the character on the hot seat questions relating to the story, and the student on the seat must answer in character. The class might ask, "Goldilocks, why was the third bed just right for you?" or "Goldilocks, what is your favorite flavor of porridge?" Goldilocks could answer: "The third bed was just right because it was not too big or too hard, and I liked the color of the blanket" or "I like blueberries and honey in my porridge, just like baby bear does." This exercise helps students draw connections between their lives and the lives of characters in the story, something that makes tales relatable and more interesting to them (Clements, 2018, pp. 159–160).

Dramatizing Picture Books: Use familiar classroom or home board books, and encourage children to dramatize and act out the stories. Simple tales such as "The Little Red Hen" or "The Little Engine That Could" provide action and plenty of fun, without complex scripts or props.

Tableaux: Students in groups freeze time at a specific event in the story. This exercise forces students to think about how characters might be positioned and what they would look like in reacting to the event. For example, a group of four students could create a tableau illustrating the instant that the wolf blows down the stick house in "The Three Little Pigs" or Goldilocks is discovered by the three bears.

If more than one story is to be play-acted on a given day, the teacher needs to be considerate of young children's attention spans.

Creative Drama

Creative drama can offer many multimodal possibilities. For example, a teacher could ask children to close their eyes and imagine that they are flying like an airplane high above the ground. Depending on how attentive the students might be, the teacher could ask them to imagine flying over mountains or rivers, deserts or forests. Students can then be asked about what they saw, felt, heard, tasted, and smelled. Activities like this encourage socialization, the use of creative imagination, language skill improvement, problem solving, and the understanding of human behavior. Children are natural multimodal players, as they use their bodies to represent characters through gestures, dance, or pantomime.

Role-playing at literacy-related play centres

Here is a small range of literacy-focused centres based on real-life settings that could be created in the classroom. Children gain an opportunity to assume roles they may have observed people fulfill in their community.

The Sports Store: In this play dramatization, children act like salespeople, cashiers, and customers. The play centre is built to resemble a sports store, with shelving, chairs, checkout tables, and merchandise. Children could measure the feet of customers for sneakers or skates, take inventory, write sales slips, and perform simple numerical calculations for purchases. This activity allows students to bring their own experiences and ideas into their play-acting and learning. In a real sports store, children would be surrounded by literacy — posters, signs, advertisements for professional athletes. They can create these materials using their prior knowledge and imagination to bring the play centre to life.

The Flower Shop: This play centre is designed to look like a flower shop. Students can create posters and signs that they would see in a flower shop to bring the setting to life. To build this centre, display a variety of plastic or fabric flowers in different-sized containers (e.g., vases, cans, buckets) on shelves or tables next to ribbons or brightly colored paper. Some flower shop play centres even have a play telephone, so that students can take and write down orders. Make sure that there are chairs and a checkout table so that the children who are playing the floral arrangers, cashiers, and customers have a space to play.

The Campground: A camping play centre needs a park station, a campsite area, and a pretend lake or river, made from paper or fabric such as a blue sheet. Children can devise campground rules, set up imaginary tents, prepare outdoor meals, and catch fish. Make sure that this play centre has literature on park events and the wildlife that lives in and around the campground. There should also be stones for a firepit, sticks for fishing poles, and camping supplies.

The Fix-it Depot: Safety should be a special consideration at this centre because it will be filled with broken appliances and toys. This play centre needs shelves to display the broken objects, tools, manuals/workbooks, and repair instructions. Customers will select items that they need repaired. The chosen repair person makes notes about how objects were repaired and issues receipts detailing the cost. As part of engaging in literacy learning, students can also make and display posters about safety, repair tips, and procedures to be read.

Authentic props will entice children to use the play centres because they make the centres seem quite realistic and tactile. Play centres and dramatic play use real-life scenarios to help children engage with literacy. Because of this, it is important that these centres include as much print as possible for students to interact with.

Literacy Materials to Use in Dramatic Play Centres

Doctor's Office: calendars, books for waiting room, telephone, prescription note-pad, posters for being healthy, instructions on how to use stethoscope

Clothing Store: labeled shelves, labeled clothing items, telephone, receipts of sale, advertising posters, notepad and pencil, cash register

Pet Shop: labeled cages with stuffed animals in them, cash registers, labeled shelves, food containers, advertisements, telephones

Hotel: telephone, magazines for foyer, notepad, receipts, maps of the area, pamphlets for future destinations, tags for hotel room door, in-case-of-fire exit map

Café: cash registers, order pad, child-created menus, list of specials, magazines to enjoy while drinking "tea"

City Hall: permits, licences, telephone, notepad, posters for local events, local maps, pamphlets for nearby areas, sign listing possible services

Museum: labeled exhibits, information about each exhibit, name tags for curators/docents, tickets, receipts of sale, books about museums, history, or natural history, posters, maps

Candy Shop: labeled shelves, labeled jars of fake candy, notepad for taking orders, telephones, pencils and pens

Zoo: labeled cages of animals with information about each animal, tickets, name tags for zookeepers, stickers to show that entry fee was paid, books about wildlife, advertising posters, maps

Antique Shop: receipts of sale, manuals for collecting antiques and comparing worth, advertising posters and signs, labeled shelves, older goods for sale, notepad to take orders

Train or Bus Station: arrivals and departures board, tickets, luggage tags, books for waiting area, safety messages for bus or train, trip location posters, name tags for station masters

"Build-a-Bug" Workshop: labeled jars of bug parts (pompoms, googly eyes, pipe cleaners, toilet-paper rolls), notepad for ordering, receipts for sale, instructions for how to construct bugs from different combinations of items, books on entomology and insect life

To be successful, literacy-related play centres, such as those identified above, must include activities that will promote children's communication and literacy engagements. The centres and props need to be relevant to the children's lives and identifiable, so that when children go to a play centre, they recognize that they are now entering an imaginary space of some sort. The physical space of the play centre also needs to be distinct from other play centres in the classroom so that students can move from one to the other without trouble. Play centres with similar themes should be grouped together. The materials within play centres need to be clearly labeled, so that children can put them away easily. These props should be relatable, authentic, appropriate, functional, and sturdy — children love dramatic play, and such objects will be well used.

The value of literacy-related play centres

Literacy play experiences using play centres and dramatic learning can be adapted to suit listening, language, and writing development. Children have a natural affinity to engage in playmaking with one another, and through this type of interaction, they will discover new information that may contribute to the development of their literacy skills. Children play characters (e.g., customers, florists, and repair people) and use the literacy props appropriate to each centre's theme. By creating authentic learning as closely as possible to the children's lived experiences, play centres foster deep understanding and positive learning experiences.

Note that before children play at the centres, the teacher should give a scaffolding session. Doing so can create a foundation for literacy learning. Janet Moyles (1989) suggests that students are more receptive to new ideas when they can explore them freely, at their own pace. She recommends what she calls the "play spiral" model. In this model, free play occurs before and after structured or more challenging play (Moyles, 1989). Children should be allowed to explore and examine materials and situations for themselves before new concepts or a lesson is introduced by the teacher. The second round of free play allows the children to master the centre to a certain degree; it also enables the teacher to assess if any and what learning has taken place (Moyles, 1989).

Free play can occur only in schools where the teacher views her role as an enabler and initiator of learning. In this approach the teacher provides vital invitations for play to develop. The play spiral model follows an inquiry-based learning model where, in this case, play centres can enrich children's literacy experiences.

Invitations to Play with Poetry

Like poets, children catalogue experiences through both facts and emotions. Poetic rhythm, imagery, and sound of words captivate children. Almost instinctively they will move to poetic language.

When selecting children's poetry, keep in mind that it should share a rhythmic language; offer an emotional appeal, exploring a variety of moods, themes, and engaging topics; and elicit a sensory delight, capturing the early life experiences of children. The poetry should have beats and patterns that coalesce in rhythm and melody. It should be both age and topic appropriate, also light in tone. Finally, the poetry should help children connect with their five senses. Children who are introduced to poetry at early stages are more likely to develop a lifelong fondness for the narrative form.

The making of poets

- Many poetry readings can be accessed through online reading programs. Have children try to deliver the same readings.
- Remember that poetry can be easily chosen to relate to topical units in the classroom such as seasons and holidays.
- Invite children to display poetry using different types of media.
- Play poetry recordings and have children follow along in well-known books such as those by Shel Silverstein.
- Invite children to act out poems such as "We're going on a bear hunt."
- Suggest that children base their writing of poems on personal objects from home.
- Encourage children to write dual poems, such as in their first language and in English.

Poetry is a unique narrative form that connects both language and art. Children see illustrations in the rich, evocative language and some find that it ignites within them a spark that can be fanned into a real passion. Children often relate most easily to contemporary poetry, but they may be well familiar with nursery rhymes through family reading at home.

Poetry and writing

If possible, invite local poets to work with children. That can be a very positive experience, connecting the children to their community, while encouraging them to create poems of their own. Here is a variety of poem-related activities for children to engage in:

- Go on a nature walk and have students collect items from it. Invite students to make a collage, using visuals to create sensory poems.
- Explore "I like" poetry, using magazines and other visuals. Invite children to share something of themselves. Doing so will help them develop opinions and build critical thinking. Examples include "I like [my favorite thing to do]" and "I like [my favorite food]."
- Encourage children to write riddles about things they see in their classroom setting. First, prompt them to find something to write about; then, have them imagine that they are that thing. Because riddles are clues that lead someone to guess an answer, all children need to do is describe what they are. Riddles are participatory, so creators can share their riddles with the class. Riddles should be no more than six lines. The last line is "What am I?"
- Make poetry stones. Students draw images on small stones and then place all the stones in a bag. Each student draws out four stones. Students create poems based on the images on stones they draw out of the bag.
- For color poems, children create collages from different materials of the same color and then write a four- to five-line poem. The second and last lines rhyme. Example:
  Blue are the waves
  That float on the sea.
  They move up and down
  Waving at me.

- Haikus are three-line poems of five syllables, seven syllables, then five syllables. Encourage children to write haikus on different themes, perhaps dinner, recess, or a favorite film character.
- Involve children in creating book spine poetry. Children gather books so that the spines face out and then arrange the spines to create a poem. Example: Goodnight, Moon. Goodnight, Gorilla.
- For concrete poems, children write poetry in the shape of their subject. For example, a poem about a flower would be written in the shape of a flower.
- There are several ways to make "Found" poetry:
  1. Children carry around notecards for the day. When they hear words they enjoy listening to or speaking, they record those words on the notecard. The poetry is then made from those words.
  2. Using patches of magazine, letter, or newspaper text, children highlight words they like and that make sense together. They then color in the spaces between the highlighted words so that the highlighted poetry is all the reader will see.
  3. Children can work with an existing poem cut up into individual words or phrases. They can rearrange the words to create new poems.
- Prompt children to pick a consonant and write as many words as possible that begin with that consonant. They can then string the words together to create a sentence. Example:
  C — cat, car, can, catch, couch, cold, cool
  The cool cat can catch the couch by the cold car.

Worth Repeating . . .

Oral language is central to children's early literacy development. The stronger the oral language base, the better the reading foundation. If we encourage children to explore and make new discoveries using talk, as well as learning through play centres and other scenarios outlined in this chapter, we will ultimately help them to understand how the functions, form, and content of the language they use to communicate are important. Playing with language builds a platform upon which children learn to decode words. When teachers build expressive language through active listening and play-based activities, it encourages students to ask questions and listen to answers in contexts familiar to them.

The explanations of how oral language develops, the play vignettes, and the planning for talk, storytelling, and creative drama contained in this chapter all encourage teachers to build their students' knowledge base and confidence about how to use language to communicate. Children come to know that words, how they are used, and the gestures paired with them, may not be appropriate in every situation. Teachers often have a vital role in helping children make these connections. Most important, by playfully encouraging children to think about the ways in which they speak, teachers build bridges to the more complex reading and writing tasks encountered in later grades.

3

Playing with Print: Towards Reading and Writing

Even before they come to school, most children know that oral language can be represented by symbols and marks on a page. Through the observation of language in use around them — environmental print — children come to understand that language appears in many forms. Children who are immersed in play-based environments can experiment with how language is used, constructing an understanding about the forms of written language, their meanings, and the connections between them. This is how they come to understand that the marks on a page have meaning in and of themselves, and that these meanings contain information of interest to them.

Classrooms that are play oriented allow time for children to experiment with and experience language; however, achieving this can be a challenge for many school curriculums, which generally rely upon repetitive skill-based worksheets. Many worksheets prompt children to practise needed skills, such as printing and making numbers. While most parents and educators agree that these skills are needed, they are also aware that asking children to learn and practise these skills apart from an active engagement with language may ultimately make it harder for them to see the connection between what they are doing and the language in use. Play can help bridge the gap between how everyday language is used and the needed foundations for reading and writing.

Immersion in Print and Social Interaction

Many language theorists have demonstrated that children come to language use when immersed in an environment both print and verbally rich — one that encourages interaction (Dyson, 2003; Graves, 1994; Hall, 1987; Heath, 1983). In a rich environment, children learn the important and needed aspects of language, including the differences between language and sound, the rules that govern language use, its varying meanings, and how to use it.

For educators and parents, the first step in developing language use is to make sure that the environment is print rich. In one visit I made to a Grade 2 classroom, the teacher had placed labels on things so that children would be accustomed to the use of words with objects to see how words can represent their visual knowledge of the world. Taking this approach is an important way to include children, particularly those whose home language is other than English, and show them words in their first language.

Many teachers adopt a similar approach. They link objects, colors, and ideas to words in print. Students' names are an ideal starting place for classroom print displays, as often they are the first words children can read or write. Taking attendance each morning is important as children begin to realize that they are accountable — that they are at school to learn! Asking children to sign in on a daily sheet suggests the importance of their names. They may find it motivational to view how others write their names and form letters. Using the attendance list to reinforce who is in school reminds children that print has a function in sharing news or knowledge in the world.

Although providing a print-rich environment will encourage language learning, children's interaction is what brings rich language learning. In other words, children need good language modeling by others; however, if they are to become literate, they also need to experiment and test out different hypotheses on how language works.

We know from research on children's play that children build language ability and skills when they interact with one another through play. In her studies conducted in Israel and the United States, Sara Smilansky (1990) found that dramatic play and socio-dramatic play both contribute to the development of cognitive and socio-emotional skills in young children. The children in Smilansky's studies showed many gains in school literacy due to their play: gains included richer vocabulary, deeper language comprehension, more curiosity about language, and better expression of ideas out loud.

The key element — the one that does so much good during play episodes — is that the situation almost always requires children to talk to one another. Children regularly come up with interesting themes and locations for their play, such as going to the doctor, visiting the vet's office, or running a café. Agreed-upon themes, such as "let's play restaurant" or "let's play school," can become the common ground for collaborative playmaking. As they play out scenarios, children describe what they are doing and show how everyday objects can symbolize other things. Basically, free play encourages risk taking through the sharing of children's ideas about what to play. Playmaking draws from the pretend world and grows within the frames of a specific theme.

Constructive play lends opportunity for the teacher to support students' language interaction. While students are engaging in constructive play, teachers have a perfect opportunity to introduce a question for them to investigate or new vocabulary words or skills. In many ways, this is a perfect type of interaction for children, one where they can, at the same time, gain confidence and regulate themselves in language ability. Imagine a trio of children getting ready to put on a rock concert: they might practise with their instruments, draw up pretend tickets, or try out dance moves. This sort of play invites the teacher to expand on what children know and scaffold in new learning by asking critical questions and providing resources.

Children's functional play contributes in the same way to their emergent literacy in writing. It may be witnessed in the early classroom Writing Centre, where children practise writing their names and those of their peers. These pretend-written forms may be letters to relatives, complete with invented spelling, or notepads filled with messages for friends. As opposed to other sorts of playing, sending notes, drawing pictures, and making lists are all writing-practice play scenarios: efforts that build towards real writing engagements. At first, such attempts may have just simple symbols to characterize letters and words, but as children notice how letters are formed and how print is used to communicate, they begin to use real letters from the alphabet to convey their meanings to others.

Following Games with Rules

Games with rules are particularly helpful when we are teaching children English language forms. Just as the games require a certain narrow interpretation of rules, so does English sometimes require a more concrete learning process. When they play games governed by rules, such as board games, children must understand how to use language forms just to get through the games. Just as important, however, they must know how to interpret the rules of the game and negotiate with others. Children begin to associate the rules of a given board game as a guiding form to find success. Whenever a disagreement or argument arises over the rules, the teacher can take advantage of an authentic teachable moment to reinforce social skills, such as playing fairly, taking turns, communicating clearly, or co-operating.

Environmental Print — Reading Our World

Environmental print is the print we see in our everyday world. It consists of the forms of language that have meaning in our environment. Sometimes called "directional print" or "signage," it is children's first reading experience of the world around them. Environmental print could be television remote-control buttons, street signs, logos, print ads, notices, magazines, notes, food packages, and catalogues.

Most children quickly come to see how environmental print symbols represent meaning. To offer a common example, many children understand street signs, like STOP, long before they comprehend any conventional text. Connecting children's first reading to environmental print builds their confidence, competence with language, and self-esteem. Most children can also readily connect meaning to environmental print because early reading experiences have already occurred in the home and in their community.

One pioneer researcher in early literacy, Marie Clay (1993), found that children often first become engaged in reading environmental print. In a study she established that children explore varying aspects of print in the home and surrounding community. Environmental print allows authentic learning opportunities for children whereby they are introduced to new word choices, spelling, and letter form — all through marketing choices meant to attract attention. Children's interest in books and print emerges due to these early connections. Children begin to form hypotheses about how letters form words and words lead to messages of communication.

Children often play-make meaning using the print they see. I once watched a group of preschool children make tickets for a community hockey game that was raising money for a hospital. One boy had a sibling with cystic fibrosis, and visiting the hospital was a common experience for him when home with his mom. Making use of the boy's experience, the children excitedly designed what they thought the ticket should look like. This artifact showed much literacy understanding, evoking both the hospital and the hockey game. The boy had tangential experience of both, enough to create a graphic impression, even though his command of real print was slight.

Often, when children enter school, parents feel as if the literacy experiences they have had may not be what is needed in school. In a session I conducted on school readiness, a mother shared this: "I am afraid we don't read to our daughter enough. Kayla can't really spell anything, and she never plays with the word-builder game we bought. She will be way behind the others." In reality, the child was neither behind nor ahead of the rest of the children in emergent literacy. The mother was following the typical popular culture message about literacy, that only conventional reading of narrative texts is literacy. I tried to reassure her that her daughter was coming to understand printed text in a satisfactory fashion and that her overall environment was fine.

In an overview of language and literacy in the early years, Terry Piper (2003) presented several factors to consider when children enter the formalized instruction of the classroom. Children grow and come to language at different stages, and their readiness for more formalized learning varies tremendously. Many young children already have a clear sense of what interests them and what does not. Their experiences of play have an impact on their language ability — social interaction is central to their language and literacy learning.

As educators, we can make students excited and curious about their world by introducing them to printed text that will help them read their world. When children first enter the classroom, the onus is on us to find out what they can do and what they find challenging. By basing literacy engagements for children on what they already know, we can empower them to include the learning they bring to the classroom. For example, children often know several logos and corporate symbols, such as the McDonald's Golden Arches, grocery items such as Froot Loops, Kraft Macaroni and Cheese, and store names, such as Toys "R" Us. On the other hand, children who have been raised in other countries and societies each develop a different mental schema for printed text, and, as such, they each have different experiences with print exposure. Their different schemas mean that these children will view print in different ways and their understandings of print may differ.

Harste, Burke, and Woodward (1984) looked at early literacy development and print awareness. In their study they found that children know a lot about print before formalized instruction begins, but early language programs often assume that children know little about it. Their study had interesting implications for teachers in that early-grade educators would have greater success in promoting print awareness if they built on the many language strategies and the knowledge that children have about print before they enter the classroom. The researchers also argued that children need to learn written language through a variety of experiences, especially those that are representative of the world in which they live. Although most researchers agree that skill-based instruction is important, the researchers advised that teachers also need to be aware of whole language theories, where language is essentially about meaning making. These theories encourage teachers to explore reading and writing from many perspectives, of which the child's environment is a crucial piece.

Children not raised in North America may find consumer symbols and print quite foreign; if so, it may be useful for you to ask their parents to situate your understanding of what early print exposure would have represented in their first countries.

Classroom Ideas for Exploring Environmental Print

Combining play and environmental print is not difficult, and there are many play scenarios in which children will enthusiastically participate.

The imaginary restaurant

This scenario can be played out in different ways, depending on what the teacher hopes to achieve. When the goal is to focus on environmental print, do the following:

- Collect a variety of restaurant and other take-out menus, or ask the children to bring them in. Aim to represent a wide variety of cuisine choices (e.g., Indian, Chinese, and Italian).
- Prompt the children to either draw or cut out photos of the foods represented; or, they could find or create pictures of their favorites.
- Invite the children to either use the existing menus or create their own.

With menus in hand, the children can role-play a variety of café and restaurant scenarios. Since the goal here is to create awareness of print, any extension of the play should lean towards print activities, such as creating snack labels, posters for imaginary restaurants, snacking guides, and simple recipes.

The local landmark alphabet book

A landmark alphabet book, based on the children's own community, is a good way to encourage both print awareness and local connectedness.

- Ask parents to help children obtain local tourist information and publications, postcards, and maps, and to share photographs that they may have in family photo collections.
- Encourage the children to identify landmarks that are important to them, perhaps a park, a public library, or a church.

Each landmark should be assigned a letter of the alphabet and then represented either by a drawn picture, a photograph, or one of the gathered printed sources. Eventually, these can be combined into an alphabet book.

This play, which calls on creative thinking, could be extended by changing some of the letters to correspond to seasonal variations in the environment, such as showing the landmark in both a winter and a summer setting. Another idea is to focus on one landmark and engage in a wider exploration of it, say, the history and environment of a popular local park. The goal is to give as much scope as possible to connect the alphabet to the children's physical environment.

Postcards from far away

This game requires planning and the co-operation of parents and other adults, but it can satisfy and interest children. The idea is to make geography more real by bringing a personal experience to the mystery of Somewhere Else.

Encourage the children to ask parents, friends, and relatives who travel or live elsewhere to send postcards with generic greetings to the classroom or give them to the children to bring to the classroom. Depending on who sends them, these postcards can be displayed on a map of the country or even of the world. By displaying where each postcard is from, you can create a sense of wonder within the child. There may be a great opportunity to teach about different countries and societies, and about the basics of writing a postcard.

Another variation is to invite the students to create their own postcards, based on either real places they have studied or on imaginary places they have envisioned. These postcards can then be filled in and "mailed" within the school.

Either activity can be combined with classroom map-making. Maps can be as simple as showing the way from the child's home to a park, or from school to home. Rather than having them draw the spaces to which the map reader is to be guided, ask children to cut out representative pictures from magazines and catalogues. For example, a tree can represent a park; a car, a parking lot.

A real-life connection: The bakery café

Environmental print can also connect classroom learning to the community, providing rich and memorable learning experiences. In Amy Wilson's Grade 1 French immersion class, students wanted to have a French bakery café modeled after their local Sobey's grocery store. The students first examined the weekly grocery flyers to understand how the grocery store is divided into departments. They cut out pictures from the advertisements and in French made signs, labels, and name tags. On their field-trip visit, Amy took pictures of the store to help the children with their choice of bakery items and bakery café design.

The children invited their parents to the opening of the bakery café, complete with a ribbon-cutting ceremony. Students took on the roles of bakers, cashiers, and servers. They stocked their café with dishes, baskets for playdough baked goods, and a cash register. The bakery café captured the children's attention for the whole year because it provided a play area and materials to which all the children could relate due to the real-life grocery store visit and family visits when the café opened.

Bridging Children's Home and School Worlds

Environmental Print Apps
AlphaTots
Montessori Crosswords
TeachMe: Toddler
Community Signs
Learn the States with Flat Stanley
Tiny Countries
State Bingo and Road Trip US

Environmental print is being used to bridge the gap between home and school in Jenny Temple's classroom. In her early literacy intervention program, Jenny uses symbolic representations to help the class create an ABC book. As part of this program, she calls upon parents to help build children's skills at home. Using objects from the children's neighborhood, homes, and school, Jenny actively involves her students as she connects their cultural and learning worlds.

Jenny initially asked parents to bring in their children's favorite books; however, she quickly noted that some did not have any books. Instead, when parents visited the classroom, Jenny chatted about reading environmental print. She offered grocery flyers, catalogues, and coupons she had received in her own mailbox and explained how these accessible resources could be used to reinforce print recognition. Parents were pleased to discover that everyday print is a good way to introduce children to early concepts of print — many of these parents had had difficulty with school as children, while others were newcomers learning English.

Environmental Print Items
- Newspapers
- Calendars
- Event brochures
- Grocery flyers
- Recipes
- Junk mail
- Food cartons

Using Environmental Print

- Use environmental print to promote a talk curriculum. Provide a list of environmental print items, and make it available for parents to help children collect items from home. Ask children to describe how they came upon these items and to share their experiences. As a group, you could create a scrapbook of children's literacy experiences to show how home and school together can become a learning community.

- Teach letters and words in contexts that define a child's world — home, pets, snacks, entertainment. Use sheets of logos that can be accessed from the Internet. Doing this can help children to understand that letters make up words.

- Active engagement in reading helps children to understand that as you do, you become. In other words, when they contribute print examples from their environment to form a personal ABC book, they are promoting literacy in their world.

Although educators are called upon to make use of environmental print, it is just as important that parents take the same opportunities. Remind parents that their homes are filled with numerous printed artifacts, all of which can be introduced to children in a playful fashion. Parents can and should use these environmental artifacts to encourage their children's emergent literacy.

Book-related play

When children play using books to provide themes, they think about social situations and problems that could arise from the real world. Pretend play through stories may be personal; while it focuses on settings or characters within tales, it always has a personal spin. Children use themes and characters from books to connect to the world around them while they play. When children create play scenarios and dramatic scenes from stories, thereby exploring literacy, they take ownership over their work. Play allows children to learn from books. It also allows children to learn about books.

Play that is derived from books is fluid as young students frequently change their minds about what they want to play or how they want to play using stories. Children create their own interpretations of books and should be allowed to do so without interference. Children consider the elements of stories that are important to them without restrictions. When students touch objects and relate them to their everyday life through gestures, movement, props, wardrobe, language, and set design, they are understanding their world through the world of books. When children play using books, they learn that there are many ways of interpretation — for example, scripts, drama, and pictures. Children thereby discover new ways to communicate and to create meaning. Young children assign roles and interact with their peers, thus creating community bonds. Even when children play-act books alone, they still reflect the social interactions that a community would provide. When children play with others, they use their peers' understanding of the world to scaffold their own understanding of the language worlds around them.

The line master on the next page provides parents with a summary of ways to promote literacy at home.

Early Literacy Practice at Home

Make literacy engagements with print a part of your home and family routine.

- Engage your children in helping to write a grocery list. Write the items down in a numbered list and ask them to help by copying letters. As they print the name of an item such as "milk," say the letters out loud: "m-i-l-k." Point to the letters of the word as you speak.

- Within the kitchen, create a scavenger hunt associated with certain letters. Ask your children to help find items: "What is a fruit whose name starts with the letter *o*?"

- Talk about how things are grouped — for example, cold things (e.g., meats and dairy products that go into the fridge) and canned and bagged food that may be kept in a cupboard. Doing this helps children to notice how you sort and classify items.

- Help your children to read their world, as well, by pointing out words and letters everywhere you can. Read traffic signs, billboards, logos, store signs, and more. Point out specific letters in each sign.

- Ask your children to begin naming common signs and to find some letters. While passing a McDonald's sign, for example, ask, "What letter does this word start with?"

- Ask your children to identify words and letters noticed while you are driving. For example, play the game I Spy while making obvious use of the alphabet so that they will look around the environment for something whose word begins with the asked-for letter.

- Ask guiding questions to engage children in conversations that promote early literacy awareness:

    1. How do you know that says "Skittles"? How do you know that says "Walmart"?

    2. What letter do you see at the beginning?

    3. What sound does the letter *S* make?

    4. Do you recognize any other letters in that logo?

    5. Can you find another logo that begins with the same letter?

    6. Do those words begin with the same sound?

    7. Are any of those letters in your own name?

Pembroke Publishers © 2019 *Invitations to Play* by Anne Burke. ISBN 978-1-55138-336-1

Language Development through Dramatic Play

One primary way in which playful learning is achieved is through a rich interactive curriculum, one in which children's interactions with one another and the environment all generate talking — and nothing encourages talking among young children more than dramatic play. From our own childhoods, we probably remember teachers trying to get us to stop talking.

For younger children, talk is an essential part of their learning. Deciding what the pretend play will be requires discussion, collaborative meaning-making, and problem solving. The drama often depends on children directly sharing what they are doing and how particular objects will serve as needed props to move the scenario forward. The drama is created from within the children's imaginative play and the talk that frames the scenario. In other chapters we have offered many models and scenarios for dramatic play — these can be easily combined with environmental print to encourage those word and language linkups.

It was playtime just after lunch in Susan Walsh's Grade 1 class. Several girls began to talk about a popular TV show, which featured teenagers winning a talent contest. Susan observed them quietly and quickly realized that none of them had seen the show in question but had heard enough about it to be interested. Cherrise, one of the class leaders, began organizing the play.

Cherrise: Let's put on our own show. I want to be the judge.
Tani: I want to be a judge, too — the one who always says bad stuff!
Kayla: I want to be on it . . . I'm going to sing. *(She gestures as a singer with microphone.)*
Cherrise: Let's make the cards. . . . We'll give out points. Let's make the cards.
Sam: Okay. Wait. We need a band, like on the show. I will play the drums. We need more —.
Mark: (interrupting) I want to be the host. I will call people out to the stage.

The discussion continued, as the girls happily organized the talent show. Other children became involved, as well. Susan noticed that no one actually performed anything — they had too much fun chatting while they organized and reorganized their show.

Dramatic play allows children to develop vocabulary and appropriate situational behavior. Teachers can encourage this development by helping students to use language appropriate for a given play scenario. For example, if the children are playing Restaurant, then there should be a menu, a chef, named food items, and so on.

When the play scenarios are predetermined, teachers may prepare vocabulary lists and place them in the appropriate play centres. For Dentist's Office, for example, you would probably want words for X-rays, toothbrushes, waiting room, and the dental chair. The more vocabulary you introduce, the more children will likely enjoy being immersed in the play, and the more opportunities they will have to use and learn new words. These opportunities also allow for children to practise their social skills, such as being patient or taking turns, and help teachers or parents to get an idea of their current vocabulary level.

Dramatic play encourages experimentation with language and promotes the understandings that letters become words and that written language allows children to be seen as writers. Dramatic play scenarios should provide many chances for reading and writing, even if the use of these skills is make-believe or rudimentary. The goal is to create an environment where these uses can later be turned into something real. As with any skill, emergent literacy requires a background, and dramatic role-play can help provide it.

Dramatic Play and Talk about It

To the observer of young children playing in the classroom, there is no doubt that, during play, children are freed from their normal roles and step into a space in which the exploration of new identities and interactions is welcomed. They are free to explore new ideas and use language to represent these ideas in ways that reality-based activities do not permit. When children play, whether through story re-enactments or socio-dramatic play — such as "playing house" or "playing school" — they talk about the course that the play will take. In the Kindergarten classroom, the observer can watch the children constructing the setting, characters, and plot lines — formulating ideas, discussing these, and accepting and rejecting the play scenario that is to unfold — both before and during the play episode.

Some researchers suggest that this type of talk about play — referred to as *metaplay* — is an indicator of children's ability to think about language and is associated with children's later reading and writing success. Because these activities provide unique opportunities for children to engage in language that is play specific and, therefore, not usually heard or used in other daily experiences, play is an important component in the design of the of the instructional environment. Play resources, including space, props, and dress-up clothes, combined with unobtrusive guidance by the teacher "to get things going," help to ensure that the opportunities for learning through play are maximized.

— Dr. Toni Doyle

There are three types of role play: domestic play, transactional play, and imagined worlds. The desired outcomes for early learning role-playing are for children to negotiate plans, interact with other people, pay attention and give response to stories, take turns in group conversation, widen vocabulary, use imagination, draw on language skills in order to enact roles and events, and use organizational skills for creating patterns, timelines, and clear perspectives. Role-playing generally encourages learning through real-life situations. Although the students may come up with interesting play scenarios, teachers can encourage creation of a wide variety of scenarios. Teachers should change the play centres or scenarios frequently and encourage all the students to assume different roles. Some scenarios may become quite elaborate and involve large groups of children; however, teachers need to ensure that all the children participate. It is recommended that students spend 20 to 30 minutes exploring, experiencing, and sharing what they know in any role-play scenario.

Teachers need to create time and space in their classrooms for role play, not only to help students practise their oral language and written skills, but to do much more. Dramatic play is both fun and interesting to children. When it is combined with other classroom goals, both the learning and the teaching improve.

Some classrooms sequester dramatic play into centres, or special corners, where props, objects, and dress-up items spark the imagination. Such centres, notably make-believe kitchens, can also be found in institutional waiting rooms, where children are likely to congregate. They do not require elaborate and expensive toys; instead, they provide a safe and secure space in which imagination is encouraged to take hold and objects are ready at hand for role-playing.

It is important that teachers help the children understand how dramatic play and a related play centre work. Some children will already know, but others will hardly understand where to start. At first, the teacher can even join in the activity. Below, Grade 1 teachers Nancy Pelley and Debbie Toope describe a literacy learning event that points to the value of dramatic play.

Supporting Critical Literacy through Role Play

In our Grade 1 classroom, we were studying the genre of fairy tales. Our read-alouds included many different versions of the same fairy tale, as well as fractured fairy tales. We began by using puppets and face masks as props, and children worked in small groups to retell their favorite tales through dramatic play. As children became comfortable with this medium of representation, they began taking control of the play by reinventing and dramatizing various fairy tales, making creative changes.

One group of children dramatized the fairy tale "Snow White and the Seven Dwarfs." In listening to their dialogue, I [Nancy] observed how they had become critical in their analysis of the fairy tale. They decided that Snow White would not have fallen for the stepmother's trick the second time and would have refused the apple. They believed Snow White to be smart because she had persuaded the huntsman to free her and had survived in the woods alone until finding the dwarfs' home. In their representation of the fairy tale, they re-created the scene by changing the ending to suit their analysis.

Another group of children represented the fairy tale "Cinderella." As they told their story through interactive play, they decided that Cinderella would not want to marry the prince because she did not want to belong to anyone. They decided that having looked after her stepmother and stepsisters, she would rather be free. In their dramatization, they reinvented the ending to suit their view of the world: Cinderella thanked the prince for finding her lost slipper and then asked her fairy godmother to lock up her stepsisters. She lived happily ever after alone in her father's house.

— Nancy Pelley and Debbie Toope

Dramatic Play Centres

Piaget (1962) argued that children use symbolic play to better understand their life experiences. Through dramatic play, children try to understand the nature of their world. Essentially, they rehearse their future roles in life. When reinforced with appropriate props, a Dramatic Play Centre can help children to use and expand their imaginations, to build upon, dramatize, and be part of that created world.

Teachers facilitate early literacy when they interact with children in Dramatic Play Centres. Dramatic play offers many possibilities for children to see how literacy informs their lives. Teachers may enter in-role as participants or as facilitators offering an opportunity to explore language in several forms. They can help develop children's literacy through asking questions, suggesting problem solving to a play scenario, and modeling the different functions of print in each centre.

Dramatic pedagogy, or teaching through the lens of drama, can be very effective with students. It allows them to be metacognitive, to think about their own thinking. It also permits students to develop critical thinking and problem-solving skills so they can assess their own work while "in role."

Creating centres for imaginative and dramatic play requires neither large sums nor great effort; however, doing so permits children to rehearse life experiences in an open-ended way. Some centres are described below.

The optometrist's office

Check with students' parents to see whether they have any old doctor or nurse sets at home. Collect small containers with lids and plastic sunglasses. Set a small table in front of a corner in the classroom, and place items in which children can record things: an appointment book, a calendar, and several clipboards with information cards for children to complete. Provide some chairs and books for children to read, as they wait to see the optometrist. Make a simple eye chart and other charts that have letter blends and words for the week. Pop one of the plastic lenses out of the sunglasses, so that children may safely test their vision and word knowledge with just one eye; or, create glasses from pipe cleaners. Create notepads for the optometrist's prescriptions. Always encourage the children to take turns role-playing: client, receptionist, and optometrist.

The museum

Before they can engage in this role play, children need to understand what museums are and what their purpose is; however, because a museum is relatively easy to set up, it is an excellent centre and a particularly inspiring play scenario when paired with a field trip to a museum. A role-play museum needs a theme that the children can contribute to and that relates to what the class is exploring, for example, birds, shapes, a form of transportation, or even individual letters.

Shoeboxes offer an engaging way to capture children's interests in this play scenario. Involve the children in making displays of artifacts or pictures, using shoeboxes as display cabinets. Children can work in groups or on their own. All items displayed should be labeled, even if you need to help with the task. Having children list their artifacts with a picture of each teaches classifying and sorting skills. You may want to display the shoeboxes for a parent night or at an annual literacy fair.

The garden centre

Creating a garden centre for children, whether in your classroom or outside, is a rewarding and holistic activity that connects children with their world. The life cycle of a plant is a popular unit in the early years, and this play scenario connects easily with those activities. Bring in seedling growing trays and introduce children to the idea of planting a garden. Let the children choose and plant seeds to help enable them to understand a plant's life cycle. Plants are observed for size, color, and texture, as children follow a step-by-step procedure. Children can be involved in spotting words on seed packs and in reading and writing plant labels.

An extension: The class could create a buying area with plastic plant pots in a range of sizes, catalogues for ordering plants, and garden furniture. Let children make their own seed packs by cutting envelopes in half. Ask children to represent language in many forms, from drawing pictures of the plants to writing names and prices of seeds. As a class, write down the growing instructions; have children copy them onto packages. Provide a shoebox where the seed envelopes could be kept according to the type (e.g., tomato, peppers, beans). Provide checklists with boxes where children can check off what they are purchasing, the number of each, and the cost. In this way children can learn about graphing and mathematics.

The café

Creating a role-play café lends opportunity to celebrate the many cultures you may have in your classroom. Decide together on the types of food to place on the menu, and invite children to share their cultural practices. In one Grade 1 classroom I visited, the teacher had found pictures of the varying cultural foods children had chosen for the menu and created the children's menu with these pictures. Parents were thrilled to see how she had included aspects of their cultural heritage, and the children learned implicit lessons about diversity. This role play offers a great opportunity to extend a unit on holidays and celebrations in a tangible way.

Ask for children's help in creating the café. They can bring in plastic cutlery, paper or plastic plates, cups, and bowls. At the same time, you can collect such items. Set up tables and seats, create order pads, perhaps find or make a phone, and place a toy cash register at the front of the café. This centre encourages children's emergent literacy because they can write in many forms ranging from the menu and price labels to posters and the sign for their café.

The veterinarian's office

For a unit on people in the local community, you might invite an animal technician to come and show the students how to safely hold and care for their pets, and to talk about the types of medical attention that animals receive at a veterinarian's office. Have children record their care of the animals during the visit.

Ask children to bring in a stuffed animal from home to serve as a pet. Ideally, a variety of animals will be represented. With the assistance of the class, make a list of animal types, for example, dog, cat, snake, and fish. Provide a registration sheet that requires children to answer simple questions about their pets. Using cardboard boxes, ask the children to prepare carrying crates for their pets and to provide items that will help meet the pets' basic needs. Provide uniforms for the veterinarian and an assistant. Talk with students about how to watch out for pets' safety and health.

The travel agency

To create this centre, drop by a travel agency and collect some brochures, posters, and pictures about holiday adventures. Encourage the children to note the different places they could visit and to make their own posters and brochures. Set out several desks and ask children to make nameplates and business cards. Provide a holiday adventure form that asks for simple information, such as type of travel and destination. Invite children to seek out informational books from the library, to find out more about various destinations. Globes and atlases help children to situate places. Students can represent different countries and regions, whether real or imagined, and offer information about excursions and attractions.

The travel agency centre and play scenario is great for helping children understand the world in which they live and for raising cultural awareness of different countries and cultures. It is also a wonderful centre to support or combine with a unit on transportation.

A Junior Kindergarten student has created a passport for use at the travel agency centre.

In the reflection above left, Kindergarten teacher Liz Macintosh shares and reflects on a group experience of imaginative play in her classroom. Such experiences offer a great way to assess children's problem-solving skills, critical thinking skills, and communication skills.

Active Engagement with Words and Letters

Teaching children to read and write is about creating a small series of links and building blocks between sounds, symbols, and eventually words and sentences. One of the first and most important links is connecting each letter they already know verbally to the visual representation of that letter, and then helping them to sound out a given word, with a focus on the initial letter.

One important theme of this book is that children must make meaning by reading the world around them; that said, the curriculum demands that they also grasp the basic tenets of letter formation. Using read-alouds, where the teacher engages the children in listening and discussion, is a way to point out certain features of print along with the connections of letters to the associated sounds. When the teacher shares alphabet books, students can learn to connect each letter to its visual form. The teacher is then able to helps students sound out a word with a focus on the initial letter. These connections are the beginning links for reading.

We want children to build understanding about their world and to use the associated language to make more observations. Using concept books to engage

Cooking Show Activity

Students, in pairs, write a short, simple script for a cooking show. They use words they already know as well as any new words you provide. The cooking activity should be age and skill appropriate, with proper safety measures kept in mind. In fact, the activity need not involve cooking. Students could follow basic recipes, perhaps for granola, lemonade, and fruit salad.

If time and ambition allow, help students set up a space, a table, relevant ingredients, and equipment (e.g., mixing bowl and spoon) in front of a camera, phone, or iPad for recording. Students practise and perform their script while cooking. They can then share the video with the class and upload it to the class website or YouTube (parental permissions allowing).

children in discussions about the alphabet and associated letter vocabulary helps children begin to understand the functions of print. Children can see the use of both upper- and lower-case letters and how the corresponding illustration of the letter contributes to their association of a letter to a certain object or concept. Concept books are important because they explore complex ideas, such as telling time, classifying, and sorting, but do so in a way which orients children to our world. Many concept books, such as alphabet books, centre on culture and customs and thereby help children to acknowledge and accept all cultures and practices.

Writing in all forms, even the simplest ones, can and should be incorporated into the play areas of the classroom. Even young children use a combination of symbols and letters to engage the beginnings of print knowledge. For example, labels made to direct children where to place things are important. To use some of the play scenarios described earlier: A container at the optometrist's office could be labeled "Pencils"; at the travel agency, a box could be labeled "Forms." These things help children to focus on how we use letters to name things.

Class routines offer many opportunities to introduce letter forming.

- During the morning message, whereby children gather at the front of the class as the first activity of the day, the teacher can create a name guessing game: "I would like this helper to come forward: she has an *S* at the beginning of her name and it has an /S/ sound as in 'snake.'" The teacher then makes the letter formation in the air. Doing so reinforces the letter–sound relationship while letting the responsibility for learning remain with the students.
- Another effort involves creating stations where students explore the formation of letters, as well as how they can connect letters to their names.
- Pass around a class list, with all names printed in large bold letters. Ask each student to circle the focus letter in her or his name or in the name of a friend.

As children learn more letters and symbols, they should be encouraged to use and incorporate these into their early writings. It is important that teachers provide scaffolding between children's imaginative play and their use of written letters and symbols.

Working with names

One of the best ways to start connecting sounds to letters is via children's own names, among the first words they hear and the first words they see written out many times. Sometimes, children will begin with just the first letter: "Look, there's an *E*, like me, Emily . . ." From there they begin to recognize other letters in their names, gradually making the connections between those letters, the sounds they make, and their names in a textual form. The first step, however, is to ensure that children recognize their names. Choose a consistent way of using each name, spelled and pronounced the same way it is used in the home.

Playing simple games using the child's own name will reinforce the link between letters and sounds, and, depending on the child's name, encourage an early understanding of phonics and spelling. Some of these games will encourage children to recognize their names and the constituent letters, while others will develop their letter–sound linkages further. (See the line master on page 68, which is written with parents most in mind.)

Name Games and Activities

Home provides many opportunities for parents to help their children learn their names. Here are some ideas to put into practice:

- Spell the child's name when you use it; talk about the sounds and the letters.

- Label some of your child's possessions, and put a nameplate on the bedroom door, so he or she sees the name used as a printed text.

- Encourage the child to sign cards and letters, even if the printing is unclear.

- Cut out letters from advertisements and catalogues. Encourage your child to use them to spell his or her name. Do the same with alphabet blocks or fridge letters.

- Ask your child to identify the letters in her or his name within the environment — look at billboards, mail, menus, and so on. If your child finds this too hard, just focus on the first letter in the name.

- Tell stories that use the child's name instead of that of the main character. Spell out the name whenever possible.

- With your child, make a photo album, and label the photographs: "Ashley playing soccer," "Ashley in her Halloween costume." Ask your child questions that will elicit answers about what is happening in the photos.

- Invite your child to work with baking and cooking ingredients, such as rice and flour, on cookie sheets to make letters of the alphabet.

- From a nature walk, you may find items such as pebbles and sticks. Your child can then use these to practise constructing his or her name.

- When shopping, ask your child to help locate letters of the alphabet that you see on labels and on signs.

- Every name is selected for a reason that becomes a part of someone's identity. For example, a child may be named after a beloved grandparent. Explain that reason to your child so he or she will better appreciate the importance of the name.

In the opening days of school, teachers may want to take the following playful approach to having students learn the names of their classmates and how to pronounce the names correctly.

- Ask students to print their first and last names in capital letters on stiff paper, name-tag size. Provide cut-outs of unusual shapes (e.g., hearts or hexagons), and ask the children to glue their printed names to a piece of colored construction paper. Do the same with your name.
- Collect the name tags and place them in a box. Have students take turns drawing a name tag from the box, finding the child who owns it, and pronouncing the name correctly. The child (or teacher) whose name tag is drawn will determine whether the pronunciation is correct. The whole class should then say aloud the name in unison.

Developmental Stages of Writing

Children's writing development is characterized by six stages. Writing begins with a basic exploration of marks on the page and then zigzags until it becomes an entrenched practice with the child producing real letters to form words and sentences. Success at this process comes in many different stages, and some children find that learning to hold crayons or paintbrushes appropriately helps them make the transition from drawing to writing.

1. *Drawing:* Regardless of skill, all children should be encouraged to draw. It will develop physical comfort with tools like pencils, but it will also create an awareness of the skill — representing something real via a graphic on a page.
2. *Scribbling, random and controlled:* First attempts at writing often result in scribbling or other drawings that are purely abstract. As time goes by, these scribbles become more concrete and begin to resemble something. Often, the child will establish the difference, dismissing one piece of "art" as scribbling while describing another as a letter to Grandma, even though the parent or educator would be hard-pressed to make any distinction.
3. *Forms that resemble letters:* From scribbling, children progress to letter forms that demonstrate a clear effort at printing. Although the results are likely to be mixed and inconsistent, the educator will usually be able to recognize the child's intentions.
4. *Letters that are recognizable:* At first, these are likely to vary widely in shape, construction, and size, with adherence to a line being optional. As time goes by and the child gains more skill, the patterns will get more consistent and the results more frequently recognizable.
5. *Spelling:* The child begins putting letters and groups of letters into sounds. Again, this process is gradual. At first the child will probably just guess, attaching a familiar sound to a spelling. As the child's skill base widens, he or she will be able to spell words with greater ease.
6. *Words and sentences:* The conclusion of this process is the ability to print recognizable words and sentences, with the appropriate punctuation.

On the next page, teacher Karen Keogh shares her success with the Flat Stanley Project, a proven and engaging way to promote writing and reading among young children.

The Flat Stanley Project

One of the most fun, hands-on, play-based activities I have ever been involved in uses a paper doll to stimulate curiosity, creativity, oral and writing skills, problem solving, family involvement, imagination, journal writing, and illustrating. In Jeff Brown's story *Flat Stanley*, a little boy gets flattened by a bulletin board and ends up as thin as a piece of paper. He discovers that he can slide under doors, becomes a kite, and catches museum thieves by posing as a picture. Best of all, he can fit into an envelope and travel all over the world. A teacher in London, Ontario, Dale Hubert, developed the idea of having children write and illustrate their own versions of Flat Stanley's story as a way of improving their writing.

Each child decides how Stanley will look. I've seen them with freckles, glasses, earrings, chains, tattoos, and a variety of skin colors. The paper dolls are laminated in case someone wants to take him to swimming lessons. The places Stanley goes will depend on the interests of the children and their families. I have often had requests for an extra Stanley for a younger sibling who wants to be part of the project, or siblings make their own.

As with any assignment, family involvement varies, but we celebrate all of Stanley's adventures. First, we read *Flat Stanley* and brainstorm the things we could do if we were flat. The project's flexibility makes redirecting it to a theme or subject area suitable for any grade easy. One year I chose "Me and My Family" as a Kindergarten social studies unit — we can learn so much about other cultures, new places, traditions, customs, other people, and ourselves through the project.

I send home a note to parents telling them that their child is bringing home a guest for three weeks. Stanley is learning all about real families and would like to be included in their daily lives. He doesn't eat much and can sleep on a bookshelf. Each child has a journal to record any three activities that the family does together. Children must include a brief description of the activity (helping to prepare a meal, going to church, playing board games, hiking, doing a puzzle, visiting relatives) and an illustration or photograph. Through stories, discussions, and visual literacy, my constant message to the children is that "there are different ways to be a family. Your family is special no matter what kind it is" (Parr, 2003). Parents often comment that they learn new things about their neighborhood, community, and province while showing Stanley around.

When the journals are completed, children share them with the class. The students talk about their favorite adventure and show their pictures. I also choose one page from each journal to make a class book that each child takes home to share with the family. As a teacher, I have a great deal of fun, too. I'll never forget the day the children came back from Music only to discover Stanley in their Easter baskets with chocolate all over his face. He was then called to the office by our principal for a time out because he took the chocolate eggs without asking!

In addition to going home with the children, Flat Stanley has had adventures overseas. He has visited many prominent members of our society as well as other countries. My Flat Stanley has seen celebrities and media figures, all of whom sent back pictures of themselves with Stanley. He has visited New York, Hawaii, France, the Dominican Republic, India, Jamaica, and Italy. My class has often received postcards from Stanley when he goes on vacation, something that usually leads to an impromptu geography lesson complete with globe and a lively discussion about what Stanley might be doing, eating, and seeing. We also talk about our postal service and the steps involved in getting a postcard from Stanley to us. Every year, this activity snowballs and brings more fun and learning to my students.

The creativity involved is limited only by the imagination of the teacher and the students. For example, for one Remembrance Day, we dressed extra Stanleys in camouflage and sent them to Afghanistan with messages for our troops.

— Karen Keough

Helping to lay foundations for writing

Making language real and writing authentic for children depends on children seeing how the task asked of them engages real communication. Providing authentic literacy experiences that frame their literacy engagements at home, perhaps going to the grocery store, subway stations, and restaurants, helps children see how written language is important to learn and use for communication with others. Modeling how to use telephone message pads, make grocery lists, and create recipes for a cooking session encourages children to use written forms in their play.

As children's scribbles begin to turn into real writing, there are playful ways to lay down a foundation for their efforts and promote a general awareness of writing in the world around them. On page 79 you will find some relevant games and exercises you may want to recommend that parents adopt.

Encouraging children's writing

There is nothing particularly intuitive or natural about the act of writing. Teaching children to write begins by acknowledging that writing can be difficult and by encouraging students to see themselves as writers. If the principles of playful learning can help them think about writing as a process, not as a problem, students are free to improve at their own pace. As with any skill, students can better develop by copying existing and possibly more advanced writing by published authors, from teacher examples, or by their own peers. Encouraging fine writing in a classroom is not easy, even if you hope students will write because they want to and not because they have to. Teachers must explore many ways if they wish to direct and guide students towards better writing.

Helping students to view writing as a cohesive and coherent process, not a series of disconnected nouns or verbs or adjectives, can let them begin to think of themselves as writers. Older students can be taught to plan, draft, revise, and edit. By following this basic structure, students learn that the first draft might not be the final draft and that it is better to create rough and generalized drafts that can later be improved. Some students might like to polish a paragraph and then move on to the next one. Teachers should recognize that every student's writing process is a variation on a theme. While the scaffolded pattern of plan, draft, revise, and edit is foundational for students to understand how and what to write, they grow and develop a process that works for them. Forcing students to follow a process that they do not find organic can prevent them from thinking of themselves as writers and, therefore, prevent them from writing.

Promoting Writing and Reading at Classroom Centres

Although infusing play-based centres with opportunities for children to use writing stimulates literacy learning, children also need more direct opportunities to learn about written language. These opportunities should stem from a school culture that celebrates and values reading. Children learn to read best when literacy is incorporated into the regular classroom curriculum. When children learn within a culture that clearly values literacy, they will develop the desire to read. To foster this culture, teachers should craft a curriculum around books and reading — a vital life skill that encompasses the whole curriculum, regardless of whatever else is being taught.

Many early-grade classrooms have literacy centres that provide physical and temporal space for in-depth explorative play with language. They thereby allow children to build the skills to become competent communicators and language users. Oral sharing, reading aloud to children, and doing activities that use print to authenticate real-life experiences — all happen at such centres. Reading aloud makes reading multi-sensory, giving students a better opportunity to understand the text and improve their retention of what they have read. Literacy-related centres include the Book Centre, classroom libraries and reading area, the Math Centre, the science and exploration table, and the Writing Centre.

Setting up the Book Centre

A special place devoted to books is important if we wish to create a reading culture with our young students. It should be an especially inviting classroom area, a quiet, comfortable space in which to experience books. The centre is meant to have a cozy feel, to encourage quiet thought, not a frenzy of activity. Pillows, a central rug, and small chairs can help create the feeling of a separate place, where children can go and take time to look at books.

Book Centre Activities

- Using *Caramba* by Marie-Louise Gay, students could write a story about an animal different from the rest of his kind. Why is that so? How does that make him feel? Students can illustrate their story or create and then describe a diorama depicting their favorite scene.
- *Gifts* by Jo Ellen Bogart and Barbara Reid is about a grandmother and granddaughter traveling. Students could explore nursery rhymes and songs from countries all over the world. The class could invite grandmothers to attend a special Book Centre day to share the book and traveling stories.
- Students could read books based in different cultures, for example, *Crabs for Dinner* by Adwoa Badoe (Ghana), *Grumpy Bird* by Jeremy Tankard (South Africa), *The Littlest Sled Dog* by Michael Kusugak (northern Canada), or *Catching Time* by Rachna Gilmore (India).
- At the Book Centre, students could finish book-related bingo cards or do scavenger hunts with designated tasks. The teacher could label books that satisfy the requirements of the scavenger hunt or bingo card. An outline of an example bingo card can be found here:
  http://bookcentre.ca/road-trip-reading-club-printables-activities.

Creating time with books allows children to see that books are to be valued. Exploring books on their own teaches them that reading is something they can do on their own. Picture books expand the imagination and also connect children to other parts of the world.

Teachers, however, should make efforts to interact with children in the Book Centre, to engage children in exploring age-appropriate books that span many genres, encompassing everything from fairy tales to nonfiction. Developing children's taste for literature takes time. Many teachers read aloud texts of a wide range of genres to their students.

Choosing the books

Teachers need to select a variety of books likely to appeal to students of the diverse range of abilities and interests represented in the classroom. Think about the reading likes of the children in your classroom and what they would want to experience. Plan to include books that may reflect the interests of children as you have observed during play; for example, after noting student interest in digging to China, a teacher put out books on China and the Olympics. Display books that may be a part of the ongoing exploration and play in the classroom.

Include a variety of genres that appeal to growing minds, for example, interactive books, such as pop-ups for children to explore as well as informational books with large pictures and organizational maps. Although many teachers and parents believe that children are more interested in stories than informational books, an explosion of nonfiction picture books attests to children's insatiable demand for books about things that interest them. Picture books, such as the popular I Spy series, ask children to develop their visual literacy skills.

As part of providing texts that interest children, choose books that are culturally relevant to the children in your group. Books should offer positive messages about different cultures and viewpoints: Take care to screen out books that offer broadly stereotypical or offensive depictions of any ethnic group, either in the stories or their illustrations. Ideally, the collection is multicultural, with titles representing the literature and characters of varied ethnic and cultural groups.

Choosing Culturally Relevant Books

Consider these questions when choosing texts intended to interest your students:

- Does the story foster the idea of valuing different cultures, linguistic backgrounds, religions, genders, and social classes?
- Do you have dual language texts that celebrate students' home languages?
- Does the story relate to the home literacy practices of your students?
- Do gender roles avoid stereotypical representations?
- Are ethnic minority characters shown in positions of power?
- Does the book have an easy-to-follow storyline?
- Does the book give insight into how people live their lives, paying attention to culture and experiences?
- Is the language appropriate and does it have repetition?
- Does the story engage the reader through interaction, such as by opening flaps?

Seeking gender balance

Books should also show some gender balance. Boys, for example, will often gravitate towards action-oriented stories, stories that feature a mischievous protagonist, or basic nonfiction. Girls sometimes have quite different interests. Strive for a balance in the depiction of roles assumed by story characters of each gender. Given the limits of space and budget, try to balance these objectives out.

A list of books reflecting gender balance appears in References and Resources on page 154.

The Book Centre as a place for reading

Reading spaces vary widely, but there are many simple and inexpensive ways to make the Book Centre a special place where children feel encouraged to read and explore literature.

- If possible, choose a corner — it is likely ideal.
- Place books flat and facing out so children can see and read the covers.
- Hold books in containers according to the genre.
- Create inviting seating with pillows, beanbag chairs, and carpet squares, or mats with children's names on them.
- Display books of early reader interest — ABC and 123 concept books, wordless picture books, predictable books (with repetitive text or text that closely matches pictures), informational picture books, and early reader books.
- Choose books that represent a variety of genres. Look at traditional literature, such as fairy tales, folktales, and nursery rhymes; nonfiction; songbooks; and realistic fiction. Books that repeat language or that have lyrical or clever rhythms are particularly attractive to children. For example, *Caps for Sale*, which applies repetition of phrases, *Silly Sally*, which applies rhymes, or *Princess Prunella and the Purple Peanut*, with its many alliterations, will provide memorable experiences for students that they may recall even as adults
- Storytelling props will help students get into the playful spirit of things — a special blanket, puppets, flannel boards with cut-outs of book characters, dress-up clothes, shakers, and musical instruments can all create ambience and role-playing possibilities.
- Make an MP3 player available, with some headphones and audiobooks.

Building a culture of reading through special events

Schools can also create a culture of reading through initiatives and celebrations. Events like these elevate the reading culture of the school and can make the prospect of reading fun. Many students do not enjoy reading for its own sake at first and must come to understand that people read for many reasons. Literacy events, which can have a lasting impact for positive change within the school, are most powerful when they have a direct purpose, such as inspiring children to read for pleasure. These one-time events might not capture the imagination of every child; nonetheless, they can be instrumental in changing students' attitudes towards reading.

Key to promoting a reading culture is to ensure that reading times for students are meaningful and authentic. Silent reading after lunch every day or a story read by the classroom teacher, for example, will help children want to read and will help them read well (Clements, 2018, pp. 85, 92–96). Here are some examples of short celebrations and initiatives to promote children's reading:

- *The Tower of Books:* In this classroom challenge, students place every book they have read either in an individual tower or a collective one. The teacher can set targets and time limits. The visual reminder of effort is very satisfying for some children.
- *The Great Reading Challenge:* Choose one author or series, and then challenge the children to read all the works in one or two weeks. Offer a small reward and encourage talk about the books.
- *The Author's Visit:* Invite a local author to visit the classroom and share his or her work. Encourage the children to read the author's books first and prompt them to come up with the most interesting questions possible.
- *Character Dress-up Day:* Have a special dress-up day where children dress as their favorite character in a book. Ask each child to describe the book and their chosen character and explain why the character appeals to them.

Library role play

Organizing the reading experience through a dramatic role play in the classroom can be very interesting for the children. Set the classroom library books available for borrowing on a shelf and use a desk for the checkout counter. Make up some cards for library borrowing. Display posters about books or prompt the children to create posters for special events. Display a message that today there will be a special visitor to the classroom.

As children become more competent as readers, you can hold book talks, where a child takes on the role of librarian and shares a book with the rest of the class. For older children, you can prompt reader response: ask for a simple one- or two-line review about why they liked or disliked a given book.

In the role of a librarian, invite the children to the book time. Ask them to suggest how they could be a good audience for the read-aloud. Present a reading in a specific genre or form of children's literature, such as fairy tales or concept books. Invite the children to read books of the same genre as the book shared. Tell them to sign out their choices before they begin to read. Involve them in selecting books for themed cardboard or plastic book boxes, perhaps titles on rhymes, fairy tales, or books about animals.

The Writing Centre

In addition to providing a good Book Centre, teachers should include space and materials for children to experiment with writing. One way to do this is to provide a Writing Centre. The youngest children often "write" using broad scribbles, which befit their level of fine motor development and their definition of writing. For many young children, writing is defined as putting marks on paper (or any other appealing surface).

Children need to understand and develop their concept of messages to further identify themselves as writers. They learn about messages through watching adults and peers or recognizing print in their surroundings. Children will explore the act of mark making and perceive messages in books and other literature. Their scribbles are similar to an infant's babbling. Just as an infant babbles to experiment with the sounds he or she can make, taking pleasure in repetition as well as variety, so do novice writers delight in discovering the infinite combination of marks that they can make. Young writers find satisfaction in gaining enough control to deliberately repeat the same marks. Thus, for the youngest children, writing takes on characteristics of both exploratory and practice play.

A good writing area encourages this playful exploration and practice. Here are some key characteristics:

- A display of the alphabet is especially helpful to those children who are ready to experiment with conventional print, moving from letter-like forms to real letters, using either invented or conventional spelling.
- Children will also experiment with the alphabet if stamps or stencils of letters are provided.
- Many children enjoy manipulating magnetic letters on small magnetic boards; after forming words that interest them, some children try to copy their words onto paper to preserve them.

Children at this age will likely seek out centre materials that facilitate the writing they want to do in support of their exploration of themes and their project work. Beyond exploratory and practice play at a Writing Centre, preschool and Kindergarten students will immerse themselves in construction: creating a piece of writing that will serve a specific and personal purpose.

Here are some criteria for creating a Writing Centre:

- Choose a quiet space away from other centres.
- Provide a round table for discussions and conferences.
- Make available pencils, pens, washable markers (thick and fine point), pencil crayons, pencil leads, crayons, chalk, glitter glue, and sparkles.
- Display an alphabet strip at each seat.
- Make available letter stamps.
- Set out magnetic letters.
- Post a list of theme-related words or create a related word wall.
- Display books related to class themes and projects.
- Make available letter and rhyming games.
- Provide paper of various sizes, colors, textures, and functions.

The Blocks Centre

A Blocks Centre is commonly found in preschool and Kindergarten classrooms. It is a simple space that utilizes blocks of various kinds. A smooth rug is a desirable feature for play. Providing vehicles such as toy cars, trucks, airplanes, tractors, and fire engines is also helpful.

To promote reading and writing at the centre, aim to provide the following resources: traffic and road signs; plans, such as blueprints for construction; pencils, markers, graph paper, and paper to produce signs for constructions; and labels for constructions of various types, such as bridge, tower, castle, and house. The list below, which reflects what educator Jane Lloyd uses in her classroom, outlines some literacy-related blocks activities for children.

Wood Blocks
Use blocks as dice with instructions.
Measure your body with blocks.
Finish a floor puzzle with blocks.
Use unit blocks to make a square.
Build towers to match photos.

Book Making

Making books is a fascinating activity for children from Kindergarten through the early grades, both playful but also offering sound literacy tasks. There are many different approaches to making books, depending on what skill level the children have achieved and what areas the class is studying.

The simplest way to make a book involves nothing more than a sheet of paper folded into four and then cut into four smaller pieces along the fold. Stapled together, they form a book of four pages. Two such pieces of paper will yield eight pages. Most children will enjoy the assembly and cutting as much as the drawing and printing.

The subjects need not be complex. Here are a few suggestions, but the idea lends itself to just about anything.

- *Number Books:* Each book focuses on one assigned number. The student either draws or procures images to represent that number or count that quantity of objects.
- *Alphabet Books:* These work with letters of the alphabet. The child either draws something that begins with the letter or seeks out images and prints representations of the letter.
- *I Can Books:* The first page starts with the phrase "I can . . ." All subsequent pages contain images of things the child can do.
- *I Would Like Books:* Similarly, the first page states, "I would like . . ." Subsequent pages illustrate activities that the child would like to be able to do.

Children also enjoy deconstructing the form of the book. Concertina books are interesting — they are made by folding a piece of paper repeatedly until it forms an accordion shape. Concertina books can be illustrated by a continuous picture, perhaps one done by different children. Another interesting book form is the strip book. A strip book consists of pages that are divided horizontally, so that the viewed page can be one composed of strips of different pages. The strips can be used to create pictures or short sentences in different and surprising ways.

Provide blocks with letters so students can spell out simple words as they build.
Make a shadow drawing with blocks.
Build a city block or an entire city.

Lego Blocks
Build letters with Lego blocks.
Spell words with letters on Lego blocks.
Create a Lego puzzle; mix and match parts of images to create a whole image.
Create a Lego maze.
Use large Lego blocks, playdough, and string as floss to teach children healthy teeth care.
Measure and create patterns.
Fill large Lego blocks with water and freeze so children can explore science concepts by playing with the Lego-shaped ice cubes.
Explore symmetry or create towers with blocks.

ABC Blocks
Spell with ABC blocks.
Print blocks in clay.
Match blocks to a larger print mat.
Build name towers.

Helpful websites for encouraging literacy skills

Beyond all the measures that teachers take to promote writing, there are, of course, opportunities for parents and guardians to do so at home. On the next page, there is a line master you could distribute to the parents and guardians of the children in your class.

Used in moderation and with parental supervision, sites such as these can provide a constructive supplement to efforts such as those outlined above. As with all things Web related, first explore any site thoroughly. Ensure that the content is positive and that games are age appropriate.

- Check out StoryPlace: The Children's Digital Learning Library.
  http://www.storyplace.org/
- Starfall helps to inspire a love of reading and writing.
  http://www.starfall.com/
- Children can enjoy games, coloring, videos, and music, and visit sites about favorite PBS cartoon characters. Visits will help children learn letters, build words, make sentences, and expand vocabulary.
  http://pbskids.org/
- The website of the popular children's TV show offers many simple and interesting games that take a basic look at letters, words, and numbers.
  http://www.sesamestreet.org/home
- This website, sponsored by the National Council of Teachers of English, helps parents encourage literacy in the home through games, activities, projects, and podcasts.
  http://www.readwritethink.org/parent-afterschool-resources/grade/1-2/

Play as Scaffolding for Literacy Success

Children benefit from a combination of explicit instruction and opportunities to play. They learn best when they can use their language and literacy skills to interact with the world and with one another; achieving this requires a degree of explicit instruction. However, it is just as important that time and space be made to allow children to play with language, with print, with words, letters, and sounds. As we have seen, they can do this in the structured space of a classroom literacy or role-playing centre and at home during casual conversation.

Society places a premium on good reading and writing skills, with both achieved as early and as fluently as possible. The environment is a vital part of furthering this process. From children's earliest steps with oral language and sounds, to their first attempts to draw letters, creating an environment that encourages playful exploration of language is simple, but important. A print-rich environment does not require expensive technology or computer toys, just a healthy and thoughtful approach on the part of educators and parents.

Either way, whatever direction we as adults give to the play, we must remember that it should reflect children's vision and interests, and work towards their emergent understandings of language and how it works. Time must be made to allow children to progress through the various developmental stages. All children learn at a different pace, and culture, gender, class, and the other perceptions and

Writing Ideas for Children at Home

Both reading and writing can be enhanced by healthy attitudes and practices at home. Although many parents read aloud to their children, there are many other ways for you to engage your children in literacy activities before and after school. This line master focuses on writing.

- Involve your child in your own writing: "Here is your grandmother's birthday card. Shall we write a little note before our names? We could say that we hope all her birthday wishes come true."

- Encourage experimentation with pencils, pens, crayons, and paper. Many children like to imitate adult work. Pretend flow charts, instructions, and whatnot can all be created using nothing more than lined paper.

- Make a storybook together: have your child dictate the words and then watch you slowly and deliberately print the story out. Encourage your child to draw pictures and fill in what words he or she can.

- With your child, write letters to friends or relatives. The child should write as much of the correspondence as possible, and then dictate the rest.

- Encourage your child to take responsibility for household writing, even if the results are not ideal. Invite your child to sign cards, help draft lists, and make labels.

- Make a scrapbook or memory book that contains samples of your child's writing and art.

- Praise the effort, but not overly so. You want your child to learn that there is a right and a wrong approach to printing.

- Resist the temptation to take over or supervise too much when your child encounters trouble. Making mistakes is a huge part of this learning process.

- Invite your child to play with toys and scenarios that involve writing, for example, writing pretend mail, making shopping lists, and filling in applications.

- Word Find is always a popular choice for learning letters and recognizing small words within larger words.

- Before taking a trip by car, bus, train, or plane, discuss words associated with the trip, for example, *luggage*, *map*, *gasoline*, and *trailer*. Write out the words together.

- Look at newspapers and advertisements that come in the mail and ask your child to copy words that seem interesting.

- Supply paint, sand, shaving foam, or rice to encourage your child to play with letter formations.

- Play a game of letter jumble with magnetic letters on the fridge. Show one small word, such as *cat*, and leave a group of letters nearby that could be used to create other words, for example, *m* for *mat*.

- Reuse cardboard boxes, encouraging your child to build something like a robot. Suggest that the creation be labeled and given a name, such as "Timmy the Robot."

Pembroke Publishers © 2019 *Invitations to Play* by Anne Burke. ISBN 978-1-55138-336-1

interests they bring to school must be taken into account. Play allows children to gain confidence and skills in a fun and engaging way: a way that reinforces and scaffolds learning without their being aware of it. Guided play also allows the teacher to gear lessons and learning to all children.

Finally, we must remember that to children, playing is their work. If the adults in their lives use play as part of their learning, and are eager and willing to participate, then the children will also see learning as part of their social and community worlds. Language and literacy are achieved not by use of a strict hierarchy of lesson plans, but by a steady immersion in a rich environment, where the children's explorations are constantly rewarded with new knowledge.

More than once the term *scaffolding* has appeared in this chapter. In this context, scaffolding is how educators create tasks that provide a knowledge base for later, more complex achievements. Using play creatively to encourage emergent literacy is all about scaffolding. Whether discussing alphabet sounds with a young child, encouraging a book-inspired role play, or providing a Writing Centre, we should strive to draw on children's natural inclinations for play to create a base for their future literacy and language success.

4

Playful Problem Solving: Mathematics

When we talk about introducing young children to math, we are referring to much more than the nuts and bolts of arithmetic. Beyond simple addition and subtraction, *numeracy* is the ability to reason with and understand math concepts as applicable to our lived lives. Many people cringe at the mere word *mathematics*, but math is not only about numerical values. Mathematics is essential in forming the world we live in; it is about life and creativity. For young children, math encompasses a whole world of problem solving, the development of logical thinking, the verbalizing of numbers, and the ways and means by which they can quantify and categorize their world. Math also offers an enormous repository of games and other play-based opportunities for learning and skill building. From the daily routines of both classroom and home — the calendar, snack time, routine lineup, and more — there abound playful opportunities to put problem-solving skills to practical use. Although many children find math boring, it need not be so, and there are ample opportunities in everyday life to explore numbers and number relationships. In math, we often figure out the worth of things. The world of mathematics is a place worth spending time.

Numeracy, which is to numbers what literacy is to text, is the natural outcome of these scaffolding exercises. Estimation, patterning, observation, seriation, and number recognition are part of children's everyday lives, and we can find numerous possibilities for playful exploration. In a digital world, these skills are vital to understanding how the technology around us works, and numeracy opens up the world of digital coding and algorithms, something that will be increasingly important for children in the years to come.

Math Concepts and the Young Child

Almost from the moment children are aware of the world around them, they begin to learn math concepts. Every day they have experiences that encourage their numeracy. Sorting by size, color, or shape is an early learning skill — blocks and cups for stacking are found even in the playpen. Even children under two years of age already understand key concepts such as the nuances between shapes or the equal division of several objects. This understanding enables them to recognize aspects by size or quantity of faces and edges. Identifying similar features allows the children to categorize objects. Are the objects the same or different? This type of sorting is essential in learning how to group objects together. Preschool activities such as sharing snacks and passing out toys develop concepts of counting and seriation. How many parents count stairs while leading a child up and down, or encourage their children to count their fingers or the number of red cars on a family trip? Either is a subtle yet ubiquitous playful counting exercise. As soon as children can articulate "yes" and "no," "one more" is likely to join their personal phrasebooks.

Research has revealed that ". . . children, even preschoolers, have surprisingly powerful everyday (informal) arithmetic knowledge" (Baroody & Dowker, 2003, p. 750). Further to this, other researchers, including Griffiths (2005), have supported the necessity of introducing math concepts as early as possible. The earlier the foundation is laid, the stronger the problem-solving skills for later success.

As is the case with print literacy, children need to become comfortable with mathematics and math concepts in the world of numbers and order before they can work with them in earnest. Numeracy must be part of their everyday lives and play, part of the creative experience that is playful learning. Two-year-olds will require a substantial amount of time and the right opportunities to explore their own descriptions of what is around them. For example, a toddler may refer to a triangle as a house. When children see math concepts as part of their world and important to meaning making within that world, then they will gain confidence in numbers and in how to express them; this, in turn, will help build a strong mathematical foundation.

Math Conversations

Before educators can communicate with children about math, the children must understand what they are talking about. While this may seem self-evident, achieving this understanding can be tricky. Beyond fairly explicit instruction by both teachers and parents, communication involves using mathematical language in a normal, everyday fashion to create a solid base of math awareness for the child.

When talking with parents, offer suggestions on where and how to build awareness of math concepts.

- At home, for example, bath time offers a great chance for application-based instruction. Children love to play with water. A set of measuring cups will provide an easy way to demonstrate the difference in measurement between a half cup and a full cup.
- Setting the table with forks and spoons allows a child to use one-to-one correspondence.
- Putting toys away can be made into a game of addition and subtraction.
- While shopping or driving, ask the child to count every time he or she sees a certain thing, such as a red car.
- Even something as simple as sharing a snack can be made into a game and an opportunity for the child to talk about numbers. For example, the adult can ask the child to give out four carrot sticks and keep five, then ask for two more . . .

Shapes, which are easily found in the home and early-grade classroom, are the basis of geometry. Street signs, for example, offer a great opportunity for guessing games: "See that sign up ahead? Is that a triangle or a rectangle?" Shapes are all around us, and when you notice them, you can also call a child's attention to them. It is important that children realize that shapes exist everywhere, and using the environment is a good way to help them grasp that concept.

A pile of classroom worksheets suddenly descending on students in Grade 1 is not the best way to help create children's comfort with mathematics.

While graphing is probably more of a classroom activity, at its simplest, it can be a great way to establish higher mathematical language concepts, such as "more than" or "equal." This is especially true when the graphing activity is shared.

In Cecile O'Brien's Grade 1 class, the children have been working on the math concept of measurement. They are asked to estimate and measure using common classroom objects. Cecile first invites the children to make hypotheses, posing questions such as "About how many of these pencils are equal in weight to these wooden blocks?" She asks students to choose three classroom objects to measure mass. After they provide an estimate of what each object would weigh, the children gather around the set of scales in the classroom to weigh the objects on their own. They then graph the objects from lightest to heaviest, showing how some objects weigh more than others or may be equal in mass. During this exploration, Cecile still poses questions: "Would three pencils necessarily weigh the same as three blocks?" "Would 25 paper clips definitely weigh more than one block?"

When children are talking and playing together, they become much more comfortable with the language concepts. Being able to "try things out" is the sign of a safe environment. The implicit instruction provided by their mutual explorations is just as likely to have a lasting effect as a similar way of explicit instruction.

Building Blocks for Math Practice

In Jane Lloyd's Grade 1 classroom, students use blocks to explore engineering, problem-solve, and discover new designs. Here are some of Jane's ideas:

1. **Can You Build It?** Have a folder full of laminated real-life building pictures. Students enjoy trying to replicate buildings with blocks. Make sure that you include the name and location of the building on the laminated paper.
2. **Use blocks to make 3-D pictures into 2-D pictures.** Jane read the book *Changes, Changes* by Pat Hutchins to her students during their geometry unit and realized that blocks can be used to tell a story. Students built stories using 3-D blocks, and some traced the outline of the blocks onto paper, creating 2-D images.
3. **Make patterns.** Students can use blocks to create patterns and designs. This activity is a good method to provide formative assessment of student learning.

When children use materials to complete tasks, they learn skills relevant to that task. For example, if students are creating stories from 3-D blocks and 2-D images, they are learning narrative forms and developing their senses of creativity and special awareness. They are also discovering the relationship between 2-D and 3-D materials.

It is important to keep in mind that even when children are using blocks or materials for unstructured mathematical playtime, they are not "wasting time." Students are still learning. Unstructured design time is meaningful because children must use problem-solving, counting, and creative skills to reach a personal goal. They must also apply knowledge already acquired about such things as space, how geometric figures fit together, architecture, and engineering. Unstructured time keeps students interested and allows them to apply new learning.

Most children are intrigued and excited by mastering simple math concepts. They are motivated to do well. Quantifying their world is one of the great games of childhood. By providing them with the means to do it, we help lay the foundation upon which much more complex knowledge will be built.

Role of questioning

As can be seen above in the example of Cecile's Grade 1 class, well-posed questions stimulate classroom conversation and are the foundation for the development of mathematical reasoning. Questions asked by the teacher must "foster in-depth inquiry, a necessary component of deeply structured learning" (Booth, 1998, p. 76). Teacher questions should also be inviting enough to stimulate the students' desire to answer them. As children share their answers, they give voice to their mathematical knowledge and problem-solving strategy. By voicing their solutions out loud, children become more aware of their mathematical reasoning which, in turn, enhances their learning experience. If the questions focus on children's "methods for constructing solutions, not simply on their answers to the problem" (National Council of Teachers of Mathematics, 2000, p. 52), posing questions and having students answer them will enhance learning for all.

Students are also encouraged to pose questions of each other. Questions from other peers require students to think deeply about the task and develop higher-order math and communication skills. Although student-to-student questions can give a teacher valuable insight into class reasoning, the teacher must carefully consider what kinds of questions the children ask to determine the underlying mathematical understanding.

The teacher can help promote positive, productive discourse by using the following types of questions and prompts:

- Please tell us about how you got 50.
- Who did it differently? Explain your process.
- Do you agree? Why?
- Can anyone explain her thought process?
- Do you understand the explanation? Show us with number cubes.
- Are there any questions?
- Does this make more sense? Why?
- Is this similar to any other problem you have seen? Where? Why?
- What happens if . . .?
- Can you make a rule for your new discovery?

Bridging Home and School with Positive Math Language

In the earliest stages of children's schooling, parents need to be intimately involved with building a foundation of numeracy. Practical activities are critical during the foundation stages of learning mathematics. Initially, children will require numerous settings in which they have free access to mathematical resources that will allow them to navigate their way through play. For example, craft sticks and plastic buttons can be used to encourage counting and patterning. Before numbers come into play, children must learn mathematics through language-based activities such as song and rhyme, art, construction, water, cooking, and sand. It is important that children become fluent in the language of mathematics. Just as they must speak and understand a wide variety of words before they learn to read books, so it is with mathematics: before children can begin to grasp higher concepts, they must understand numbers and their relationships to the physical world around them.

This scaffolding and bridging process has a few key components. It may be helpful to explain to parents how children learn, using the ideas presented below to stimulate discussion.

- Knowledge is created in children by interactions with the environment and their community.
- Children go through many stages as they build their knowledge, from basic concrete understandings to more abstract thinking.
- School uses a developmental instructional approach, where children are constantly building on previous experiences.
- Children's thinking is engaged by the discovery of patterns and relationships between numbers and their world.
- Children should learn to communicate their growing understanding of numeracy in both verbal and written fashions.

Parents should understand that their involvement is vital for their child's future problem-solving abilities. Although most teachers will already know that students with engaged parents do better, it is useful to reinforce that parents' active participation will help strengthen the numeracy knowledge base upon which children's later learning will be raised. Open communication with parents about what their child is doing in math helps parents to become more involved in their child's mathematical education. Sending home examples of what students are working on in class also helps because parents gain a better understanding of what their child is learning.

First, however, the teacher may have to combat some of the parents' own misconceptions and prejudices about math instruction. Parents may already be aware that math instruction is very different from when they attended school. Many parents will recall with dismay their own math experiences and will be nervous about taking an active role in their children's education. It may be helpful to remember these common math misconceptions:

- Math is just about sums, times tables, and other exercises.
- The only way to learn math is by repetitive worksheets.
- Only some people are good at math — boys are better at it than girls.
- You need to be a teacher to understand math.
- Math is the hardest core subject.

Building Numeracy in Kindergarten

Building numeracy in the early grades utilizes a great resource, namely, children's natural curiosity about the world, and their need to quantify it in logical and sensible terms. To some degree, if children are given the right tools, numeracy will be intuitive. If we are to take advantage of this natural tendency and need for order in a child's worldview, we must provide games and activities that are within their developmental capacity and that they can use and understand.

In Kindergarten, good teachers introduce math concepts gradually, using hands-on centres and active problem solving, keeping the explorations as tangible and tactile as possible. As a rule of thumb, early numeracy in Kindergarten can be divided into four distinct areas:

1. *Number Sense:* The first stage of numeracy, *number sense* refers to establishing what counting is, as well as ordering, comparing, and establishing the relationship between the printed symbol of a number and the quantity it represents.
2. *Patterns:* Children recognize the patterns in the world around them and begin to use numbers to quantify them. Ideally, they will use this knowledge to begin predicting the solutions to problems and what happens next in a pattern.
3. *Measurement:* Children learn to compare objects on the basis of length, capacity, mass, or amount. Part and parcel of this is the ability to describe measurements and the differences between various measures.
4. *Numeracy Development:* This term refers to the ability to put all the above aspects together. Children should solve problems on their own, show an understanding of cause and effect, identify similarities and differences between things in their environment, and demonstrate a clear understanding about the links between printed numbers and actual amounts.

Good Kindergarten curriculum planning includes all the above areas, with everything building towards numeracy development. When planning lessons and classroom activities and games, teachers will find it helpful to offer parents and caregivers the advice presented on the line master "How to Help Your Children Do Math."

Planning guidelines

In the classroom, there are many ways for teachers to encourage playful and exploratory approaches to math and numeracy. Many of them use children's natural desire to learn, guided towards logical processes.

- Ask questions that are open-ended and encourage mathematical thinking.
- Use games that encourage co-operation and require children to talk to one another to find solutions — oral language is very important.
- Integrate mathematical and numeracy language into other learning areas such as science and social studies.
- Use activities and games that offer more than one solution to a problem and require some degree of critical thinking.
- Incorporate gross motor activities with math. Getting children up and moving facilitates the learning of concepts such as addition and subtraction, as well as shapes. It also makes math fun! Have children group themselves using their bodies according to numbers: "Form a group of five and make a triangle." "What if we need to show the four corners of a square? How many people do we need?"
- Give children opportunity to talk about their experiences and discoveries through a sharing time. Ask them to describe what they did on the weekend. If they went shopping at the market, they could talk about how much and what foods were purchased; if they took a drive to the cottage, they could talk about the shapes seen along the way. There are many ways to have children consider how numeracy defines their everyday lives.

How to Help Your Children Do Math

- First, become involved in your children's learning. Since all teachers are interested in extending children's school knowledge to the home, don't hesitate to ask questions, perhaps for an example to illustrate a math concept. Be sure to understand the curriculum goals, and keep abreast of classroom activities. Doing so will help you feel like much more than a homework supervisor.

- Children need to see that math can be both interesting and fun. Small games, such as Snakes and Ladders, Bingo, I Spy, and Pick-up Sticks, everyday questions, and helping-out-around-the-house activities can all promote math learning. They also provide great opportunities to make math fun.

- Numeracy is the ability to express math concepts and reasoning. It involves applying numerical symbols in ways that help us quantify our world and experiences. Be sure to model numeracy, drawing on aspects of your environment. Children need to see you use math in a practical sense. You might say: "Let's see. There are five people eating supper tonight. How many forks, spoons, and knives do we need?"

- Share opportunities to meet mathematical objectives with your children: "How many houses are between us and the Stop sign? Let's count."

- Counting or 1-2-3 books can help children gain an understanding of numbers. Children can learn to count the number of objects on a page and group according to characteristics (e.g., size and color). Find examples from your family life to help children connect to the learning from any number book you use.

- Make use of nursery rhymes and poems. Many of these use numbers, as in "One, two, buckle my shoe" or "Five little ducks went swimming one day." Counting rhymes empower and spark interest, helping early learners connect numbers to their quantities.

- Choose magazines that feature brightly colored pictures to encourage counting and the basics of addition and subtraction.

- Make math a part of your everyday chores — the idea is to develop mathematical ideas through language. As you or a child tidies up, count the items. Use the toys in the toy box in several ways, perhaps asking, "How many pieces of puzzle are you holding? How many do I have in my hand? Let's see how many blue toys are in the toy box. Which toy is closest to the television? the door? How do you know? Can you show me how?"

- Use language to develop children's math concepts about counting and comparing. Examples: how many, more or less, greater or smaller, longer or shorter, higher or lower, heavier or lighter.

- Encourage understanding of direction and position. Work phrases such as these into your conversation: in front or behind, up and down, top or bottom, next to or beside, before or after, inside or outside, over, under, and below.

- If a child answers a math question incorrectly (e.g., $2 + 3 = 6$), don't immediately correct it or tell the child the answer is wrong; instead, ask the child to explain the answer and the thinking behind it. Doing so provides an opportunity for modeling the correct thinking and the use of manipulatives so the child can come up with the correct answer.

- Avoid expressing any negative attitudes about mathematics. If you are positive about math, chances are your children will be, too.

Pembroke Publishers © 2019 *Invitations to Play* by Anne Burke. ISBN 978-1-55138-336-1

Playful Approaches to Numeracy at Home and School

A play-based approach will help children relate numbers, measurement, patterns, and equations to their environment. During the early years, the adult will lead the play to a higher degree, asking questions and demonstrating the scenarios. As the children get older and their numeracy grows, they will begin to take charge of the play, and co-operate and communicate more about the problem solving. The key to developing numeracy is asking questions that will spark the children's thinking.

The line master on pages 91 and 92 outlines natural ways for parents to involve children in math at home.

Play-based activities for late preschool and Kindergarten

Activities in late preschool and Kindergarten will allow great scope for exploring mathematics. Children are a little older and more sophisticated; more important, perhaps, they are now in a social environment. This environment is conducive to interaction and co-operation, giving children opportunities to talk about and explore their numeracy together. Children are constantly on the go — running, jumping, walking, climbing, and so on. While the Internet and teacher guides offer thousands of worksheet possibilities, the activities described here will involve children in more hands-on processes:

Pasta Sorting: Play a sorting game featuring different kinds of pasta. Give each child or team a selection of different pasta shapes, and then have them sort them by shape, size, or type. Doing this allows for children to inquire about shape, texture, sizes, and materials. Similar games can be played with beads or counting chips.

Nature Walk: Take children on a walk outside or through a nearby park. Look for different patterns or different numbers within nature, for example, five petals on a flower or a spiral pattern on a pine cone.

Math Bingo: Create a simple bingo game for younger children. Give each child a card with about 20 numbers on it, from 1 to 10. Spin a wheel or turn up cards, and then call out the numbers. As you do so, the students cross out the appropriate numbers on their cards. The first student to cross out all of them shouts, "Bingo!"

Class Matching: Play a game of matching cards on a large scale. Each child in a group holds a card with a shape on it and either turns it upside down or keeps the shape hidden. Elsewhere in the class is another child with a matching card. A third child (or group) must match the children and shapes by asking questions about the shapes without using shape names: "Is your shape like a box?" "Can your shape be used as a baseball diamond?" "Is your box like my eraser?" "Is your shape round?" "Does your shape look like a winter tree?"

Tic-Tac-Toe: This game can be made into a group activity by simply drawing the game on the board and dividing the children into small teams required to decide on their move together. Tic-Tac-Toe is a good game for patterns and logic.

Simon Says (With a Math Twist): Like many other simple children's games, Simon Says can easily be given a mathematical slant: "Simon says touch your knees together three times . . ."

Singing Games: As at home, nursery rhymes and other children's songs are well suited to numeracy. Rhyme helps children to develop numerical sense. "Baa, baa, black sheep, have you any wool? Yes sir, yes sir, 10 bags full . . ., 9 bags full . . ." And so on.

Number Tag: Each child is given a sheet or card with a number on it from 1 to 10. One child, designated It, stands in a corner unable to see the rest of the children. The child calls out numbers from 1 to 10. Each time a number is chosen, all the children with that number sit down. Eventually, one child should be left. That person then becomes It.

Red Rover, Come Over: Play the old-fashioned game, but give it a numeric slant. Each child is assigned a number between 1 and 10. The caller stands opposite the children and says something like, "Red Rover, Red Rover, number 7 come over!" Any child who has been given the number 7 tries to cross the floor without being caught by the caller through a tap on the shoulder. The game continues with the calling of numbers until the caller has captured every player.

What Time Is It, Mr. Wolf?: Children line up at the back of the gym. When they ask, "What time is it, Mr. Wolf?" Mr. Wolf responds with a time, such as 10 a.m. The children must take 10 steps towards Mr. Wolf. After repeating the question-and-answer pattern three or four times, Mr. Wolf yells, "Supper time!" The students race to the back of the gym to avoid getting eaten. Children love to play this game, and it promotes body control and counting.

Guess the Number: A teacher or a student chooses a number that others have to guess, providing a helpful clue: "My number is 2 plus 4."

Finish the Pattern: Create a classroom maze using desks and chairs. A group of children need to solve simple problems to progress through it.

The Estimation Container: In this simple but intriguing game, children estimate how many objects are in a container. Both groups and individuals can play it.

Morning Routine: Even activities such as the daily calendar and the days of the week can focus on numeracy. For instance, children can count how many days are remaining until a special event or holiday. Students can also become aware of how many days they spend in school versus how many days they spend at home.

Math with Jelly Beans: Give each child a handful of various colored jelly beans and ask math questions. For example: "How many yellow and red jelly beans do you have?" If they wish, children can then eat the jelly beans as a special "math" treat!

Who Has . . .? I Have . . . ! This game involves the use of task cards on the math topic you are currently covering. Students will read out their card and ask "Who has . . ." whatever is on their card. The student whose card has that will then read out the "Who has . . ." on their card. Example: "I have 4. Who has 3 + 3?"

Play-based activities for the early grades

By Grades 1 and 2, students are beginning to have a much firmer grasp of numeracy, which will allow the teacher to plan more elaborate games that require greater logical and reasoning skills, or a higher degree of collaboration.

The Lemonade Stand: This game requires some props, including cups and fake money, and would work well in a dramatic play centre. Essentially, two or three students run a lemonade stand. Their prices are fixed, but each customer places a different order. The stand-holders are required to figure out how much money they need to charge or how much change to give back. This activity can be made as elaborate as desired, depending on the students' ages and capabilities.

Measuring the Classroom: This rainy-day caregiver's classic also works well in the classroom. Instead of a ruler, use paper clips or craft sticks. A child lies on the floor while other students use as many paper clips or sticks as necessary to measure the child. Most Grade 1 and 2 students will enjoy counting (and recounting) the paper clips to determine the child's length. The game can also be extended by, for example, having the class figure out room width measured by number of children.

Class Fractions: Make three groups of students: one with two students, one with four, and one with six; then, ask the other students fractional questions: "How many children in the second group have to move if one quarter of them need to return to their desks?" The result will be some confusion but also a memorable lesson for the children, who will be both amused and engaged as their peers become mathematical equations.

Classic Board Games: Older children who can understand rules will enjoy straightforward board games such as Trouble, Snakes and Ladders, and possibly Monopoly. These games require significant counting skills, as well as basic addition and subtraction.

Circular Objects: The geometric principle of circumference can be difficult to explain. Getting the class to estimate and then measure the circumferences of objects such as globes, soccer balls, hockey pucks, and drink containers will make for an illuminating exercise.

The Vote: Involve the class in a vote — perhaps on the name of a stuffed pet. A good idea is to ask the students for about 10 names and to list them on the board. Each child votes using a simple piece of paper and placing the ballot in a container; then, the vote is recorded beside the names. The class identifies the top three names and votes again. After the voting is over, the class can work on simple graphs to explain the results.

Cards: Simple card games, such as War, Snap, Old Maid, and Crazy Eights, teach children how to recognize numbers, as well as do logical sequencing.

Play-Based Math Activities for the Home

Building a numeracy foundation at home requires making math and numbers part of the everyday routine of chores, play, meals, and other household activities. Parents and caregivers can readily take advantage of the numeracy already part of everyday life.

Getting Dressed: Ask young children to count everything they will be putting on. Play a timing game, counting the seconds as they get dressed. When they are putting clothes away, ask them to make patterns of socks and other garments in a drawer.

Meal Time: Ask questions like "How many spoons are on the table?" Ask for help setting a table. "There are four of us eating. Can you find a fork for each of us?" Reverse the questions to encourage the child to think: How many of us will eat tonight? How many glasses should I put out?

Snack Time: Count snacks: "I think you have three carrots left. Is that right?" For the picky eater, divide a piece of hard fruit, perhaps an apple, into different shapes: "Can you eat a round piece now? How about a piece shaped like a triangle?"

Playtime: Expensive technology is not required in order to make numeracy-enhancing games part of a child's playtime.

- Matching games that use simple cards, either store-bought or handmade, fascinate some children and provide a great example of patterning and prediction.

- Stacking cups are cheap and easy to find, and for the very young child they will provide great patterning and comparison games. Numbered blocks will do the same; for example, one might ask the child to make a tower of three or four blocks, starting at one block and going up.

- If the child has a playmate, ask them to play a guessing game: "How many beads do I have in this box?"

- Hide and Seek requires counting, as do simple board games.

- Crafting is a good activity for play-based numeracy — craft sticks and pipe cleaners can be made into many things, but also can be counted, compared, and categorized.

- Although coloring might not hold children's attention, sorting crayons by size or color might.

Bath Time: For many children, bath time is the highlight of their day, a chance to have the undivided attention of an adult and to play around with soap and water. Plastic cups of different sizes will create many opportunities to explore measurement.

Pembroke Publishers © 2019 *Invitations to Play* by Anne Burke. ISBN 978-1-55138-336-1

Play-Based Math Activities for the Home (continued)

Around the Home: Digital clocks provide a useful demonstration of numbers in a home. Many children enjoy simple counting games involving household geography: "How many steps to the washroom?" "Let's count the stairs while we walk down them." Sorting out cupboards and drawers — a lot of fun for many children — creates opportunities to play with measurement and patterns. Ask the children to put the pots in a row, from biggest to smallest. Perhaps they could figure out which pot would make the most soup. Prompt the children to use a ruler to measure household objects: "What's the tallest thing in the house? How wide is the door? Whose shoes are bigger — mine or your dad's?"

Singing: All children love to sing, whether with a parent or other children. The fact that music and mathematics are linked is common knowledge. The patterns and sequences required in music are elements of mathematics. Children commonly pick up of these aspects of music, as can be seen in their rhythmic body movements. Toddlers react to musical stimuli, enjoy shaking noisy objects such as rattles and percussion instruments, and interact through finger rhymes, dancing, and song. Many songs can be adapted to include a numeracy component or turned into a counting game. Familiar songs, such as "This Old Man" and "Old MacDonald Had a Farm," are ready examples, but a simple Internet search will provide many more.

The World Record Game: Establish record times for minor household chores and then challenge children to beat them: "The house record for putting shoes away is 38.5 seconds. Can you beat that today?" Besides getting chores done, the game teaches children time and how to recognize its passage.

Measuring Height: Make a height chart, perhaps on a door, and get the children to measure themselves against it once a month.

Outside the Home: Shapes can be sought and discussed on a walk or drive: "What shape is that sign?" "Do you see anything round right now?" Counting can also be part of a walk: "How many steps is it to the sidewalk?" The local park will provide a good place to play: "Let's pick up five pine cones — which one is the smallest? Which one is in the middle?" "Who is swinging higher — you or Rachel?" "Let's hop to the slide. Who can hop the most? Let's count."

Pembroke Publishers © 2019 *Invitations to Play* by Anne Burke. ISBN 978-1-55138-336-1

Count on Spelling: This newer game combines both literacy and numeracy. Children have a limited time to guess the numeric value of a word — to count the letters and then add them up. In other words, "classroom" equals 9; "books" equals 5. This game is good as an oral exercise: the teacher reads the word, and the class then figures out the numeric value without seeing the word printed.

Children's Literature and Learning Mathematics

Although it may not seem obvious, children's literature can provide helpful introductions to math concepts that can create wonderful opportunities for future learning. Children's literature creates inward experiences for young children: experiences that help build connections between their lives and world. There are many books and stories with mathematical themes that can assist children in making sense of numeracy. As they read, children form ideas and can grasp the math concepts to which they are introduced in unobtrusive and unique ways.

Children's books can offer explicit and implicit mathematical themes in a non-threatening tone, contextualize mathematics to the children's lived world, and encourage children to discuss, talk about, and investigate math concepts in reflective and meaningful ways. Many books have been written specifically for children learning math concepts, featuring characters and stories that make math problems an essential part of the plot. For example, simple stories such as "The Three Little Pigs," with its counting elements, is a perennial favorite. More elaborate books may offer themes about fractions and multiplication.

Many other classroom activities and learning opportunities, such as writing, drawing, and drama, can also be used to help children conceptualize math and numerical concepts. The more diverse the exploration and presentation of learning, the more easily children learn precise mathematical symbols and the language necessary to express those ideas. As they observe math concepts in action in their books and through other classroom events, these concepts become solidified and quantified for them.

When children experience authentic mathematical discovery through children's books, they unconsciously integrate content, processes, and skills from other curriculum areas, which, in turn, provides a richer learning experience and deepens their understanding. When books and stories ask them to make observations and predictions, children are also learning how to engage in meaningful mathematic inquiry. Books and stories can connect children's numeracy concepts to other subjects and to their own lives in a way that could never be grasped via worksheets. Books that connect content and strategies in a meaningful and natural way, challenge the intellect, help make sense of the world, inspire inquiry, and support and extend concepts and understanding are tools that children can use to gain detailed understanding of math topics that can unite skills from across multiple disciplines (Kiefer, 2007). Simply put, good children's books can make math relevant.

Numeracy Apps and STEM Toys

Coding Apps and Programs for Children
https://turtleacademy.com/
https://www.codecademy.com/
https://www.playcodemonkey.com/coding-adventure/
https://www.khanacademy.org/
https://code.org/
https://www.tynker.com/
https://scratch.mit.edu/

In the digital age, math and numeracy education is no longer confined to endless worksheets and quizzes. Of course, skill and drill methods remain popular and will continue to form a large part of most children's educational experiences. However, there are many apps and other digital tools that can enhance and expand upon children's numeracy. They can even create a foundation for the math that underlies digital concepts such as coding and social media algorithms.

Math lies at the heart of all computer programs and thus at the heart of all digital technology. Children learn language by connecting sounds to words, and then words to objects and actions. Although coding can be very complex, children can learn basic aspects of it and then expand upon this learning as they move further into the school system. Toys, also, have evolved to help children understand complex topics such as computation, numeracy, and mathematical literacy. Specially designed and engineered STEM toys focus not just on teaching children how to "think like an engineer," but also to give them experiences that require creativity, perseverance, learning from failure, and evaluating effective solutions.

STEM toys

STEM
S   Science
T   Technology
E   Engineering
M   Math

Nintendo Labo: This innovative toy combines maker ideas with cardboard cutouts and basic computer technology, so that children can create their own digital toys.

Brackitz Pulleys: Students create drawbridges, zip-lines, or escalators. Students can tinker, problem-solve, and apply both mathematical and scientific thinking.

SmartGames Snow White: This activity encourages young children to apply logic. It unites imaginative play and problem-solving skills. Children use critical thinking to keep Snow White and the Seven Dwarfs away from the wicked witch.

Elenco Snap Circuits: Children learn to create working circuit boards to make lights flash or sounds beep. The game teaches them about creative solutions to open-ended problems, perseverance, and learning from failure, as well as the basics of how to make electric circuits. Snap Circuits requires basic coding skills and a high degree of problem solving.

Osmo Coding Jam Game: Students connect and arrange blocks to create musical compositions that an app animates. The game teaches spatial reasoning, computational logic, and critical evaluation.

Clue Master Game: In this game, students must correctly place tokens on a grid based on an incomplete set of clues. They need to deduce where the tokens should go. This game teaches logic and helps develop important reasoning and inference skills required for more advanced study in mathematics, engineering, and science.

Cozmo: Based on a character from the Disney/Pixar movie *Wall-E*, Cozmo is a robot that children can program to move about and command to perform certain tasks. Cozmo is designed to express emotions and will exclaim gleefully, groan, or work helpfully with a child to solve problems and complete tasks. Having a buddy like Cozmo to help teach coding principles and problem solving serves to remind students that learning can happen collectively.

Cubetto Coding Toy: For the basic programmer, this toy uses blocks to program a robot. It helps children understand the basics of coding before they can read, teaching introductory lessons about sequence, order, and patterning to create a set of commands with a tangible output.

Think & Learn Code-a-Pillar: Early learners can pull the toy apart and put it back together to create a series of commands that dictate where the toy will go. Young programmers can learn about order and sequence, problem solving, reasoning, and observation.

Makeblock Neuron Inventor Kit: Children will enjoy the versatility of this activity, whereby they can do such things as programming lights to flash or making gadgets. Some children experiment with electrical current by creating a program that allows a small current to flow through people. The inventor kit incorporates math, science, physics, and engineering together and allows the student to digitally create, experiment, and explore with the tools around.

STEM toys allow students to literally "play" with math and numerical ideas. While most of these toys do not offer algorithms or equations to solve, they do teach skills that students need if they are to become better mathematicians: perseverance, reasoning, how to learn from failure, logic and inference, and problem-solving skills. With these skills and resources, a child will find learning mathematical skills similar to the process of playing with STEM toys — fun.

Coding and Robotics

These ideas, offered by teacher-librarians Gina Brown and Karen Pragnell, are mainly appropriate for students in Kindergarten and in Grades 1, 2, and 3.

- Introduce your students to **coding** (the language used to make computers, software, websites, or apps work) without using a computer. Students take turns giving directions that other students follow by using their own bodies: forwards, backwards, right, left, up, down. Do this activity on a 100 mat, classroom story carpet, in the gym, or on the playground.
- Add the words for the three basic logic structures in coding:
  selection (essentially what is your decision in which way to move)
  sequencing (how one action you take leads to the next in an order)
  looping (a particular order of instructions which repeats)

Understanding can be further consolidated in time by using coding apps and websites, such as Kodable, Box Island, Lightbot, CodeCombat, Code.org, Tynker, and Scratch.

- Follow up with a Scaredy Squirrel adventure based on one of Mélanie Watt's popular stories for any of her mapping/obstacle scenarios. After reading the story, each student will receive a paper divided into squares. Each child decides where to place an *X* on the paper as "the end" and then draws in a variety of obstacles based on the story in the squares on the way. The challenge is for a friend to describe the route using introductory coding language to reach the *X* at the end. (First, you go forward right, right, right; then down left, left, up, right, down . . .)
- Pinterest, Teachers Pay Teachers, and other websites offer simple directional-arrow line masters that you can copy, cut out, and laminate to create reusable arrows. You may want to read a fun pirate story, use the same page divided into squares, pass out jewels and tiny pieces such as Lego or dollar-store items, and have your students create a treasure map. Share with classmates and have them place the arrow cards on the squares to show how they can reach the jewel!
- These activities lead nicely into using Kodable, the app or website, where you can register your class. Your students can progress with games from Kindergarten to writing and reading JavaScript (essentially, the programming language of the Internet).
- Introduce and celebrate Computer Science Education Week each December. Visit https://hourofcode.com for all kinds of great introduction-to-coding activities from Frozen to Minecraft.

Now, take those coding skills and add some robots to the mix . . .

- Some popular robots for young children include Code-a-Pillar, Code & Go Robot Mouse, and Bee-Bots. Many come with curriculum ideas. Check with educators and parents, search the Internet, and visit tech stores for feedback.

- Wonder Workshop Dash and Dot robot kits are suitable for Kindergarten to Grade 8 students who enjoy operating the robots using apps such as Go and Wonder. Students can apply their new coding skills using the Blockly app. There are also accessories, such as the rocket launcher or xylophone, to meet mathematics, science, and music curriculum expectations.
- Lego EV3 robots cost more but can be used with Kindergarten to Grade 3 students (with support from learning buddies or Robotics Club student leaders) to Grade 8 and beyond. Lego Education apps and websites offer many opportunities for building robots and operating them using computer programming skills.

— Gina Brown and Karen Pragnell

The Role of the Math Centre

The Math Centre encourages children's learning through exploration and discovery, offering materials that will create and encourage mathematical explorations. Materials should vary with children's ages and experiences, but allow children to playfully explore numerical processes, such as sorting, classifying, comparing, fractioning, and measuring. The Math Centre should encourage play and learning subtly and non-explicitly, so that children come to the concepts naturally.

Children need a hands-on approach in order to build mathematical reasoning and critical understanding of how mathematics is very much a part of their everyday life — they do not come to understand numbers naturally. As teachers, we must provide activities that illustrate various understandings about math, keeping in mind that the relationships between these ideas are often abstract. Successful numeracy programs require children to put numbers, counting, and measurement in the contexts of their lives.

Children exploring math need to do problem-solving tasks. Because these tasks might not have a prescribed set of steps that lead children towards answers, children should be encouraged to develop their own strategies, building upon prior knowledge. As Lev Vygotsky argued, teachers need to provide scaffolding for children's discoveries from exploring, reasoning, and resolving problems through interactive play-based activities, and this concept is as true of math and numeracy as it is for reading and writing. When exploring numeracy, children should always feel safe and understand that all their ideas count. Risk taking lends opportunity for scaffolding to take place on the part of the teacher.

Having time for play and exploration helps children see how mathematics is connected to their real lives. Ultimately, it will help them appreciate the value of the math concepts. The use of playful tools and games, as discussed in this chapter, will enhance the learning styles of many children.

5

Scientific Play as a Form of Exploration

One of the most satisfying and successful ways to use play as an educational platform is through the exploration of science. By its very nature, science is hands-on and enhances curiosity in children. With subtle direction, children can come to learn, and prepare to learn, in a wide variety of ways. And they can do so while playing in ways they find highly interesting.

Scientific reasoning is a logical process, developed through a number of key learning experiences: experiences that can be a part of either guided or free play (Howe & Davies, 2005). Although some of these experiences are more important than others at various stages, all are inherently part of the most basic scientific explorations.

The skills and experiences that children can absorb from scientific play range from the basic to the complex. They include the following:

- predicting
- recognizing the importance of curiosity about the world
- problem-solving
- showing environmental sensitivity and responsibility
- charting and writing down information and findings
- becoming aware of life and life cycles
- demonstrating logic and a sense of cause and effect

Offering opportunities for children to explore explaining, demonstrating, predicting, thinking, and solving problems, as well as show creativity, is important. Strategies such as prolonging naturally occurring opportunities in the environment, planning activities with a practical purpose, fabricating adult-based activities to facilitate observation and assessment, and asking open-ended questions are all good ways to empower a child. Teachers may want to create an "I Wonder" wall for each new unit. As students have questions, they can write them on a piece of paper and stick them to the wall. As students investigate and learn, they can remove the questions that they think are now answered.

Discovery through Play

Children's play that deliberately includes scientific experimentation and exploration will reflect and develop its goals from the experiences listed above. The main goal of the play is for children to gain a love of discovery. Although they will find learning to keep records, validating ideas, and recognizing logical processes invaluable, these outcomes are secondary. In essence, we want to open children's minds to possibilities. Especially for younger children, it may be enough for us to encourage the belief that the world is something that can be explained, changed, or marveled at.

We can, of course, narrow that rather lofty goal into a few key areas: exploration, discovery, creativity, and problem solving.

For the children, scientific *exploration* is a science-oriented activity in which an outcome is not easily predicted. Although it may be possible to make a prediction about the outcome, the outcome is not one readily obvious to the child. The absence of specific outcomes or tasks is the key aspect of exploration. Such activities encourage the child to be open-minded, with freedom to discover how any number of things and processes might work.

During scientific play that involves *discovery*, children acquire specific knowledge and understanding. Not every episode of scientific play will lead to a discovery; that said, it can be a powerful motive towards more detailed and elaborate activities.

Creativity should be found in almost any kind of scientific play. When provided with the right tools and circumstances, children will be able to see events from changing perspectives, make surprising connections, or alter their previous understandings. They should be able to alter the play so that they can reach their own conclusions or alter events to create their own outcomes. Either way, fostering an open-minded approach to science and to life in general can be a positive outcome of such play.

Finally, by its nature, scientific play produces and enhances *problem-solving* skills. Children learn to identify a problem, figure out what question to answer, discover ways to go about answering the question, try various solutions, and then decide which solution worked the best — or the worst. Problem-solving skills also involve original thinking, as well as exploration, discovery, and creativity, as discussed above. While problem solving is crucial to science, it is also valuable in most other aspects of a child's growing mind. If children can discover ways to answer their own scientific questions, they are well on the way to becoming first-rate creative thinkers; they are also likely to gain enhanced self-esteem and a general enthusiasm about learning. Widening vocabulary through sustained shared thinking, critical thinking, and embedded creativity is an approach that incorporates innovation in everything we do.

In the reflection below, Kindergarten teacher Susan Barron describes how two of her young students tried out a few possible solutions to a problem that concerned them.

Wanted — A Lost Frog: Problem Solving

I observed two little girls who were searching for a little toy frog known as Froggy that had become misplaced somewhere in the classroom. The girls were very worried about the toy frog and began to ask their friends questions to see if they could discover his whereabouts. This strategy proved unsuccessful, so they decided to make up little posters with Froggy's picture on them to pass out to their classmates, in hope that seeing a picture would jog their memories and Froggy would be returned. The pictures they drew were quite detailed, but again, they were not able to bring their friend back safely.

> I remember thinking to myself that this is great imaginative play, which demonstrated genuine effort to use the new skills they had. They are talking and listening to each other, and are writing and drawing things (such as maps and posters), which have a real purpose and meaning for them.
>
> — Susan Barron

Subtle differences between very young children and their elders should be kept in mind when establishing goals for scientific play. In the earliest stages of their education, children begin connecting the dots between the elements of their worlds with the help of basic science. Specific *how* and *why* questions are not really the point; instead, we try to help them realize that they can ask questions, solve problems, or begin to make connections between themselves and the world. Sensory information and personal explorations are invaluable. Older children, or at least those who have developed more organized thought processes, can use more knowledge-based experiments. Chemical reactions, static electricity, and the surprising effects of physics are best left to them.

For any age, however, educators and parents should focus on a couple of basic principles. First, the activity should accomplish something. Activities that demonstrate why something *doesn't* happen are unlikely to fulfill any of the above criteria. Second, activities that in some way relate to the child's own observations of life and nature are more likely to have some lasting positive effect.

For very young children, these activities are not designed to fit a curriculum goal other than stimulating their creativity and curiosity. For those in Kindergarten and the early grades, the activities can easily be routed towards more concrete goals. Whenever a student asks a question about why something works the way that it does, you can easily design a simple hands-on experiment whereby students can develop the knowledge for themselves in a concrete manner. Even the simplest of experiments will enhance children's abilities in observation, classification, quantification, communication, and inference. All these opportunities will not, and cannot, be present in every science play; however, over a term or a year, all these skills can be readily enhanced through enjoyable and interesting scientific activities.

How to Introduce Hands-on Science

So, having decided to introduce a scientific element into children's play, where does the educator start? Making use of a common-sense understanding of young children's learning styles will quickly eliminate many areas of exploration. For example, anything dangerous is out, as are activities that require a lengthy wait or a long list of successive ingredients. Young children are impatient and self-centred. While they often have expansive imaginations, they are not given to abstract thinking. Easily distracted, they are far more excited by doing something than by having it explained.

Educators, therefore, should be steered in their scientific approaches by the following guidelines:

- clear objectives
- simple, clear instructions
- hands-on experiences
- easily attainable results

Heuristic play, which promotes motor movement and development, is a classic play activity that involves toddlers in exploring real objects in their environment. A mix of container-like objects and small items allows small children to interact with different shapes and with sizes and similarities. It encourages creative thinking by giving the opportunity for multiple actions. Tins, boxes, bottles, corks, shells, thimbles, and so on are tools for toddlers to interact with their environments; the interactions will develop their confidence in regard to being able to do things on their own and for themselves. The traditional nursery rhyme "London Bridge Is Falling Down," with its focus on falling, is an example of heuristic play.

Water, ubiquitous and easy to come by, offers a host of scientific possibilities for children of any age group. Preschoolers may enjoy doing simple experiments demonstrating how water can be transformed into ice and then back into water. Kindergarten students can perform experiments that use water to play with concepts about mass and volume, say, how an object's material affects its flotation. Primary students may benefit from, and understand, more complex ideas, such as how water can be used as a force for movement, through something like a simple homemade water mill.

Whatever the topic, it is important to adopt the child's perspective. As soon as concepts become too complicated, the play will be abandoned. *Keeping it simple* must be the watchword. And we must never forget the key element of any play experience: fun. If the play gets dull or obviously educational, the delight and wonder offered by scientific play will be lost.

Apples, Apples, Apples Activity

Students in Kindergarten and Grade 1 are required to explore the senses. In her Grade 1 classroom, Jane Lloyd uses provocations to help them make connections between what they already know and possible future learning. Apples are one material she has used to help students explore all their senses.

First, Jane invited her students to explore apples using sight, touch, taste, smell, and hearing. She asked guiding questions to help observation.

Next, she had students pick a favorite apple. Students colored a paper apple that was used to create a class bar graph to show which apple was the most popular. During this time, they talked openly about their observations and discoveries. Some children had never tasted a green apple and used the class activity to do so. Other students were reminded of familiar places or people because of the taste or smell of certain apples, while a few just loved the crunch of the apples.

During this unit, Jane made sure to emphasize safe ways to pick apples and how to determine when apples are no longer safe to eat. She timed this project to coincide with Halloween so that the class could talk about candy safety.

Thematically, the more the scientific activity relates to other aspects of children's lives, the more it will likely resonate in their learning later on. Effective teachers know that a few good themes, repeated regularly, work better than a huge number of ideas. For example, to use the water theme from above, in the winter the children could play with snow, which the teacher could relate to an indoor experience, such as melting ice-cubes. In April, spring rains could be brought into a water-related environmental theme. In either case, experiments could be as simple as discovering how quickly snow melts or as complex as measuring the effect of rainfall and erosion. The key elements in the success of the play will be the educator's patience, the sensory experience of the play, and the way the play stimulates children's natural curiosity and sense of discovery.

Encouraging expression

Within early years practice, science can play a significant role in developing children's participation in talk and self-expression. Gelman and Brenneman (2012) assert that a key element in promoting the development of reasoning, observing, thinking, talking, and working scientifically is encouragement.

Educators should adopt encouragement strategies intended to support children's expression, exploration, and critical evaluation — many young learners find these challenging. Discussions that centre on tactile objects or shared experiences like stories, while meaningful and engaging starting points for encouragement, are only one way of many that children use to express themselves.

In many cases, allowing students to take a multimodal approach towards expression is fruitful. Modes of expression that differ from language can allow children to demonstrate their thinking in alternative, sometimes richer, ways. For example, observations about size, sound, relative position, and movement might be revealed in drawings, gestures, actions, or models but be impossible to express in speech.

Children also need social opportunities to practise and develop their skills. To encourage social interaction, the learning space should be non-judgmental and open to expression regardless of an idea's accuracy. Instruction should be conversational and non-confrontational. Teachers should be aware of how their verbal and non-verbal cues influence what children express and how they express themselves and their ideas.

Engaging early learners in scientific discussion means giving them some agency over their explorations, helping children realize that they have ideas of their own, convincing them that those ideas are interesting, and urging them to accept that others' ideas and perspectives may differ.

The Discovery Centre

Play scenarios based on scientific principles and discoveries need not rely on expensive equipment or technology. As most parents can testify, children are often as fascinated by a stack of blocks as they are by an expensive video game. Play scenarios depend on the imagination.

Many preschool and Kindergarten rooms incorporate what is known as a Discovery Centre. Best located near a window and a water source, it is a special space intended to encourage creative and discovery play. It should be big enough to allow at least a few children to co-operate or play in a parallel fashion; it should also be sturdy enough that spills and messes are easily dealt with. Based around a large table set at a child's level, it could incorporate the following items:

- containers for water
- sand or soil, pebbles or gravel
- small plants with chopsticks to anchor them
- tools for measuring, such as cups and spoons
- sturdy magnifying glasses
- string and fabric

- shells, pebbles, or small blocks
- small tools, such as rakes and shovels
- magnets and small metal objects
- soaps
- feathers and small Styrofoam shapes
- cookie cutters
- sponges and colanders
- plastic tubes, small hoses, and straws
- food coloring

Resources for Teaching and Learning Science

https://www.startalkradio.net/category/playing-with-science/

http://littlemisshypothesis.blogspot.com/

http://www.nsta.org/elementaryschool/

https://www.pbslearningmedia.org/subjects/science/

https://undsci.berkeley.edu/

https://edheads.site-ym.com/

https://www.plantingscience.org/

http://www.smithsonianeducation.org/scientist/

https://www.youtube.com/scishow

http://mscassidysclass.edublogs.org/

www.sciencefix.com/

www.rundesroom.com/

wondersinkindergarten.blogspot.com/

Of course, all materials need to be safe or big enough not to be swallowed. These materials can be changed regularly and should lend themselves to repeated or multiple use. Encourage children to recycle and to bring in useful household materials, such as toilet-paper tubes and plastic bottles, for the centre.

Once the centre is set up, it will not take long for children to gravitate towards it. If all you have on hand is water and soil, the centre will already be irresistible to just about any child to whom getting wet is a passion. With a subtle hand, children can be easily pointed towards any number of scientific experiments. All activities should involve a basic question that the child can answer independently through physical involvement in the play. Although the centre serves as the base for such scientific experiences and experiments, these can also occur in other spaces.

Science Play: Types and Examples

Children's natural curiosity is an invaluable educational resource. While just about any scientific principle can be explored to one degree or another by children, here are some areas that particularly lend themselves to school and preschool classrooms.

Measurement play

Measurement activities can be interesting for the smallest children right up to those in their primary years. Children perform and repeat an activity in various fashions, ideally measuring the differing results. Small children can play with simple questions, older ones with more elaborate ones. Measurement activities push babies and toddlers in their exploration of size, shape, and speed differentials.

A common play scenario asks which container holds more of a given substance. Using containers of different sizes and shapes or transferring water from one container to another will be fun and instructive for preschoolers. Older children might be intrigued by exploring concepts of displacement — for example, measuring how a heavy object causes more water to spill from a container than a bigger, lighter one. Comparing and contrasting various objects and their properties can be turned into a guessing game or one involving blindfolds for an amusing sensory experience.

Other measurement scenarios involve time and gravity (keep the terminology to a minimum). Little boys love racing toy cars. A simple raceway made of cardboard tubes can be used to demonstrate concepts of weight and speed. Whose car goes faster? farther? Why? Time can be measured by making a chart about when the sun sets each day, a fascinating subject in more northern places.

Temperature offers a myriad of measurement possibilities. Sun and shade can be examined by leaving objects in a sunny window. An ice cube can prompt discovery in several ways: How fast does it melt? How much water is left over? Does the ice cube feel the same to different parts of the body?

Provocations Take You Places!

It might seem odd that writing can be taught through play. Sometimes, though, it just takes a little science. In another Grade 1 lesson about the senses, Jane Lloyd wanted her students to focus in on the sense of touch. Jane laid out objects to explore and a book about the sense of touch.

Students worked together touching objects and writing words on index cards to describe how the objects felt. Some students went back for more cards to write more words.

The next day, Jane repeated the activity. Students were still interested and even read through all the words in the basket to come up with ones that they had missed.

Physical science play

Many adults find physics to be a difficult and intimidating part of their education, but young children need not find it so. Simple concepts can lead to productive play scenarios. Such play should focus primarily on movement and the relationships between moving objects. It will thus enable children to connect keywords with objects and actions. As children change their actions, they should be able to see a similar change in the object or the object's relations to others. It sounds complex, but the play itself can be straightforward, educational, and lots of fun.

Scenarios are limited only to the child's capacity for fun. For example, twirling a basket of fabric around can teach children about centrifugal forces. The first time they do it, everything falls out. As they twirl the basket faster, everything stays in. Gravity can be explored by dropping objects: What falls faster — feathers or plastic toys? What rolls down a slope faster — a big ball or a small one? a heavy one or a light one? When children handle and control objects in such play, they also learn coordination.

Friction is a difficult concept to explain, but one that children grasp easily when they experiment with it. What moves faster along a floor — rubber sneakers or stockinged feet? How can you make something more slippery or sticky? Pushing and pulling are usually a source of parental and educator frustration, but they can be turned into a useful experiment, too. How many children do you need to pull a slippery object? What about a rough or heavy one?

Water is particularly useful for demonstrating physical properties in a playful fashion. Older children can build small pendulums or maybe water wheels from simple craft supplies. Filling an old coffee can with water and then getting children to punch a few holes in the plastic cover will provide them with a good demonstration of water pressure. Sponges allow them to explore principles of absorption. Soap bubbles are an endless source of fascination.

Biology play

Children are fascinated by the workings of their own bodies. Biology-related scenarios can be based around the Discovery Centre or take place elsewhere in the play space.

While such issues need to be handled sensitively, differences in hair color, height, shoe size, and so on can be measured and compared. Hands and feet can be traced and then compared every month. Cheap magnifying glasses can be used to examine skin or other natural objects.

At snack time, children can compare how different food tastes or feels in their mouths. Ask them to plug their noses while they taste their favorite foods — do they still taste them? Even cleanup time offers opportunities to explore questions: Why does soap help clean dirty hands? What makes our hands dirtier — sand, soil, or flour?

Environmental play

The environment offers endless possibilities for scientific experimentation, for almost all age groups. A Discovery Centre can easily incorporate ecological materials that allow interesting play scenarios.

Almost all preschoolers have at some time planted seeds in a cup and then waited for the seeds to grow — common scenarios like this can be expanded and altered in many interesting ways. To use the example above, different seeds can be used, or seeds can be planted in different materials (e.g., sand, clay, regular soil, or gravel). Transparent containers can be used, so children can watch roots develop. Plants can be exposed to the sun in different ways. Children can experiment with fertilizer or even introduce bugs. In all cases, teachers should encourage the children to make up their own minds about what is happening and to reach their own conclusions. Although these activities require patience and time, the children involved will find them satisfying.

Other environmental lessons can be gained through play scenarios, too. Simple experiments that imitate weather effects, such as water and soil erosion, are easy for children to set up and fascinating for them to undertake. Older children can set up mini-ecosystems, perhaps something like an earthworm farm in a large jar. The development of such systems is diverting and imparts important lessons about life cycles. This approach draws children into a wider understanding of the interdependence of life.

Chemistry play

At its heart, chemistry is the exploration of how substances interact, combine, and create new substances. Not many educators or parents, however, are eager to address chemistry experiments, particularly for young children: there is the stigma that *the experiments could be dangerous.* Although many people believe that young children cannot participate in chemistry play, there are many safe chemistry experiments and kits and toys that children can use to interact with this branch of science.

Young children enjoy doing simple chemistry experiments, easily repeated, with cheap and readily obtainable materials. For example, on the Internet there are recipes for "slime," using liquid food starch and white school glue. Once children add food coloring, foam balls, and glitter, watch their delight at combining disparate materials into something else entirely. Another favorite involves adding vinegar to baking soda, creating a mini-volcano. Some children make oobleck, combining cornstarch and water, and watch in amazement at how this "nonNewtonian fluid" can be liquid when gently touched and then solid when smacked. Not only does this encourage language development, but also hand–eye coordination. It is important to enlighten parents on this fact.

Simple non-cooking recipes can also show how substances of a disparate nature combine to form something useful, or at least different. Children's silly side can be engaged by checking different materials for absorbency — say, a piece of denim versus a diaper, or water versus ketchup. Remember, as with the rest of our examples, the more the experiments relate to the children's lives and the more fun they have, the greater the likelihood the lessons learned will be remembered. Asking children to add salt to water to get small objects to float teaches them about buoyancy. Dissolving sugar in water with some string encourages the growth of rock candy, a tasty and interesting chemistry experiment.

In the feature below, Christine Maclean, an early childhood consultant, reflects on the role of encouragement and opportunity in the development of creative problem solvers. She also reinforces the need for students to develop problem-solving skills.

Chemistry Experiment Videos

Slime without Borax:
https://www.youtube.com/
watch?v=jWqNK-BGRz8

Fluffy Slime:
https://www.youtube.com/
watch?v=PTu9lZcao0c

3 Awesome Science Experiments:
https://www.youtube.com/
watch?v=W6NQ_GAIZyk

Kinetic Sand, or Cloud Dough:
https://www.youtube.com/
watch?v=hVN1DsIS5T8

Butter Slime:
https://www.youtube.com/
watch?v=GizyCKSAlps

The Benefits of Open-Ended Play

When my own child was around five years old, he spent the better part of a day watching and collecting snails while he played outdoors. Later in the day he asked me to help him draw a snail. Ordinarily, my first response would be to show him how to do it, but, for whatever reason, this time I didn't. I asked him to try it himself, and then I sat back and watched what happened. He made several attempts to sketch the spiral shape of a snail shell, each attempt becoming more and more complex and each time becoming closer and closer to a recognizable snail shape. I felt like I was able to see those little wheels spinning in his head as he figured out how to solve this problem. He ended up with an accurate representation of a snail but, more important, he ended up with a sense of real accomplishment because he was able to solve his problem by himself.

He has since grown up to be a wonderfully creative artist and an innovative problem solver who has learned to rely on his own ability to generate solutions to life's situations. I'm not saying that every child who is able to figure things out for himself will grow up to be an artist or an innovator, but I can guarantee that if children aren't given opportunities for open-ended play, there won't be nearly the number of artists and innovators that this next generation will need in order to deal with the multitude of problems inherited from our generation.

— Christine Maclean

Construction play

Construction work enables children to determine the links between size, shape, and space. Building blocks, for example, often lead to sophisticated understandings of object comparisons; thus, it is not strange for a five-year-old child to have the ability to construct complex creations. Building blocks also allow children to learn scientific concepts pertaining to cause and effect. There is little intention to the creations that children make using building blocks initially, but as development progresses, children display the ability to have a vision, and they plan accordingly to make that vision come to life. Play with building blocks allows for many authentic teachable moments about gravity, shape, structure, balance, and more. Construction play brings together hand–eye coordination and manipulation of objects.

Outdoor play

The playground, yard, or park also makes an excellent site for scientific play. Here are examples of outdoor play that may lead to further explorations:

- Playground games, such as tag, can be altered to include scientific principles. For example, a group of children could form a solar system, even including comets and asteroids!
- The swings and slide can be used to measure the effects of gravity, with different-sized children involved in the tests.
- Through outdoor collecting games, where they gather items such as pebbles, wildflowers, and different leaves, children will learn about their environment in a playful way.
- The playground is a perfect spot for experimenting with paper-plane designs, materials, and propulsion.
- On a snowy day, invite children to examine snowflakes, perhaps looking for ones that are the same . . .
- Make a sundial out of sticks and stones to tell time.
- Smell different flowers. Which ones do the children like or dislike?
- Construct a long-distance phone from paper cups and a lengthy piece of string. Playing with this is as interesting to children now as it was a hundred years ago.
- Set up a backyard weather station and record daily temperatures and rainfall. Ask: "Are they the same as elsewhere?"

Children love to explore and play outside in "the wild." They are often eager to tell their parents, family, and friends about their adventures, which enhances engagement in language and communication. If educators recognize children's love and include science ideas in the play, the play will be both effective and resonant. The possibilities are endless. Engagement with nature offers lessons about patterns such as seasonal changes, animal migrations, phases of the moon, rotation of the planets, life and death, waterflow, metamorphosis, and, now, climate change. Nature brings forth problems to solve and questions to answer. How can a plant stand up straight in the wind? What causes the leaves to change color? Experiencing the outside world gives rise to symbiotic behavior and problem solving.

Science in the early years is about experiencing the physical world in many forms. It is a hands-on, discovery process of learning, whereby children come up with their own suppositions about what they see. Through play-based learning centres, such as the Discovery Centre, children can engage all their senses to communicate both their feelings and understandings.

Many studies suggest that children are becoming disconnected from the natural environment due to urban living, technology, and generally busy lives. This disconnect, in turn, can become a disassociation with the natural world and inhibit their curiosity and questions about the world. Although the limited space, time, and resources of the classroom may make science play a challenge, the benefits to children in becoming creative risk takers and problem solvers make it well worth the effort.

There are many ways that children are inspired to play outdoors even while using screens. GoPro cameras allow children to record and share their experiences from a first-person perspective. Orienteering, with compass and map, or geocaching, with a phone app or GPS receiver, turns being outdoors into a game. Children enjoy actively searching for new treasures or figuring out where they are and where they need to go.

A list of children's books about nature and science appears on the next page.

Books about Nature for Children

- *Every Autumn Comes the Bear* by Jim Arnosky
- *Why Do We Need Bees?* by Emily Bone
- *The Wonder Garden* by Jenny Broom
- *The Curious Garden* by Peter Brown
- *The Mermaid and the Shoe* by K. G. Campbell
- *The Great Kapok Tree* by Lynne Cherry
- *The Road Home* by Katie Cotton and Sarah Jacoby
- *Outside Your Window: A First Book of Nature* by Nicola Davies
- *A Walk in the Forest* by Maria Dek
- *The Snail and the Whale* by Julia Donaldson
- *Planting a Rainbow* by Lois Ehlert
- *The Night Gardener* by Terry Fan and Eric Fan
- *Eddie's Garden and How to Make Things Grow* by Sarah Garland
- *Seeds, Bees, Butterflies, and More!* by Carole Gerber
- *The Little Gardener* by Emily Hughes
- *The Big Alfie out of Doors Storybook* by Shirley Hughes
- *An Egg Is Quiet* by Dianna Hutts Aston
- *This Moose Belongs to Me* by Oliver Jeffers (also, *Here We Are* and *Stuck*)
- *Fabulous Frogs* by Martin Jenkins
- *Beyond the Pond* by Joseph Kuefler
- *Can You See Me?* by Ted Lewin
- *Finding Wild* by Megan Wagner Lloyd and Abigail Halpin
- *Where the River Begins* by Thomas Locker
- *Dream Animals: A Bedtime Journey* by Emily Winfield Martin
- *The Little Plant Doctor: A Story about George Washington Carver* by Jean Marzollo
- *Over and under the Pond* by Kate Messner and Christopher Silas Neal
- *Goodbye Summer, Hello Autumn* by Kenard Pak
- *Seed, Soil, Sun: Earth's Recipe for Food* by Cris Peterson
- *Strange Trees* by Bernadette Porquié and Cécile Gambini
- *We're Going on a Bear Hunt* by Michael Rosen
- *Nature Anatomy: The Curious Parts and Pieces of the Natural World* by Julia Rothman
- *A Whiff of Pine, a Hint of Skunk: A Forest of Poems* by Deborah Ruddell
- *Because of an Acorn* by Lola M. Schaefer and Adam Schaefer
- *Tree: A Peek-Through Picture Book* by Britta Teckentrup
- *Owl Moon* by Jane Yolen
- *The Big Book of Bugs* by Yuval Zommer
- *Our Tree Named Steve* by Alan Zweibel (illustrated by David Catrow)

6

Childhood Digital Literacies

Technology is ubiquitous in the daily lives of young children today. It is not unusual for children as young as three to master iPads or tablets and cellphones, update and use programs like Netflix or Spotify on the television and laptop computer, or play quite elaborate video games. Toy stores are full of electronic games (many touting dubious educational outcomes), while any gathering of children will find at least a few fully absorbed by hand-held video games, like the immensely popular Nintendo 3DS or Switch. At the same time, almost all parents and teachers are uncomfortable with the amount of technology in children's lives, and most schools and child-care centres have strict rules limiting device use, as do many families and homes. Even the proponents of digital technologies have reservations about its utility for children. Steve Jobs, the late president of Apple, famously would not let his children use any of his own company's digital devices.

If, however, technology is used in moderation and with mindful and guided supervision, it need not be a threat or a hindrance to educational progress. Digital tools offer new avenues for acquiring knowledge, skill sets, and the knowledge base necessary for children's future in a technological era. Technologies can also offer children a fun and lively accelerated process for learning. Parents can readily use the technology in the home to create playful scenarios that are both enjoyable and instructive. As educators, we cannot overemphasize this point: we all have a responsibility to help children become comfortable with technology, so that they can learn to use it properly and safely.

Modern researchers suggest that while tech-based tools can offer children numerous sorts of learning, educators must use the digital systems in such a way as to encourage higher thinking. Handled properly, iPads and other screen-based technological tools can enhance children's cognitive development. The key is finding play scenarios in which children are active participants, learning through the play; they must do more than passively working their way through endless levels of pointless games or sitting hypnotized by YouTube videos. We must accept that iPads, cellphones, and other computer-based technologies will remain a significant part of children's lives — the challenge is to find ways to use them both thoughtfully and in moderation to help meet children's educational needs.

How Children Interact with Computers

Getting children to interact with technology is not difficult — almost all children love to play with computers — but understanding *how* children interact with computers is harder to do. Educators need to understand how children learn when they encounter computer programs and their like and keep these learning processes well in mind when directing children's computer interactions. Researchers Jane Davidson and June Wright (1994, p. 81) have divided the learning process into four stages:

1. *Discovery:* The child experiences a growing awareness that what appears on the screen is what the child has created or selected.
2. *Involvement:* The child becomes motivated to learn and master basic commands and sequences.
3. *Self-Confidence:* The child learns to complete plans and to predict outcomes.
4. *Creativity:* The child can invent solutions to problems, design challenges for others, and even create original scenarios.

As children move through these stages, whether in the space of five minutes or a year, they are in a very real way learning to use computers as tools, just like a box of crayons or a bag of construction blocks. If we as educators think this way, we will be better able to successfully create a space for computer use in children's play.

Educators and parents will also realize that close supervision must be an important part of any such play experiences. We cannot expect children to use any discretion, find safe and stimulating play scenarios, or monitor their time interacting with technology. Although many studies emphasize the positive side of computer games, almost all also agree on a policy of moderation. Hours spent interacting with a screen provide no substitute for other sorts of play. To use a metaphor, you would not feed a child exclusively on one type of fruit or vegetable; neither should a child's play be dominated by the computer screen. Software and websites must be carefully chosen, to be both stimulating from a play perspective and full of positive messages and useful learning moments.

Bear in mind that every child will be different. Some children will easily master games and sites that require strong literacy skills; others will be more visually oriented and will gravitate towards games that flatter those skills. As we all know, boys and girls are often drawn to very different types of play, and, as is the case on the playground, so will it be on the screen. All these factors need to be considered before letting children engage with digital technologies.

Video Games and Their Benefits

A popular myth is that video games and the like are just plain bad for children; however, studies by child psychologists suggest that *what* children are playing on the screen is a much more crucial measure of good or bad. A widely cited European Union study, which looked at young children in a diverse group of demographics, concluded that "video games can stimulate learning of facts and skills such as strategic thinking, creativity, cooperation and innovative thinking, which are important skills in the information society." Games that promote positive social, emotional, and intellectual outcomes, enjoyed in moderation and not to the exclusion of other types of play, are likely to be no more harmful than any other sort of play. Since the same cannot be said about violent and aggressive games, we will focus our attention here on positive play situations.

My work in digital reading and children's play in virtual worlds points to some of the benefits and sense of reality that can come from playing computer games. A few years ago, many children became obsessed with Webkinz, a virtual world created for children. The purchase of a small stuffed toy gave them access to the website and a small virtual pet, which required children to log in for daily feedings, games, and general care.

> *Seven-year-old Adam was talking about feeding his family's dogs, a simple chore he much enjoyed, when suddenly his happy-go-lucky features clouded over.*
>
> *"We have to play Webkinz today," he said urgently. "We need to feed our animals. They will be getting hungry too."*
>
> *It had been several days since we had entered the virtual world of Webkinz together, where his small collection of stuffed toys seemed to lead a real existence. As part of the game, in a given session, players assumed the identity of one of the toys from their own collection of toys. Feeding these animals a virtual treat was a treasured part of Adam's computer play.*
>
> *In Adam's mind, the needs of his fictional Webkinz pets were as urgent and important as those of the family's real puppies.*

Children's suspension of disbelief operates on a very different plane than that of adults, as does their sense of time and urgency. Therefore, as teachers and caregivers, we must shoulder a heavy responsibility for monitoring video or virtual world game use.

Discovery-Oriented Computer Play

Several studies agree that discovery-oriented programs are often the best choices for computer play. These programs involve children in step-by-step play and are open-ended in terms of their outcomes. Historically, such programs were the preserve of expensive software games. Today, computer games are divided into two categories. In the home, they use dedicated computers, like Sony's PlayStation or the Nintendo Wii. These units offer a wide variety of games, almost all of which require the user to become part of an immersive environment. Educational outcomes are often implicit. In the classroom, anecdotal evidence suggests that conventional educational software is being steadily supplanted by online games or downloadable apps, which offer a wide variety of free play opportunities.

These programs will often exist in self-contained virtual worlds, known as "micro-worlds," which operate with rule structures and precepts easily understandable to children. These worlds, often tied to a popular TV show or toy, contain games and interactive activities aimed at children from several different age groups. While not explicitly educational, many of them call upon basic literacy and math skills, and many tasks require the child to understand responsibility and imitate life skills. The repetition of the game frequently allows the child to gain virtual money or other credits, which then can be used to alter the game's physical makeup, open new levels, or acquire virtual prizes. Even very young children are fascinated by this make-believe economy, where they can participate actively in a way impossible in their real lives. In the game, they have total control of their avatars (alter egos); while playing they are able to make choices and discover how these choices can be both positive and negative.

As illustrated below, my research with seven-year-old Adam describes how some of his choices led to an unwelcomed consequence and a life lesson.

While Adam and I were playing on a virtual shopping app, in which he could purchase items such as an online puppy, I was distracted by a message from another researcher. For a few minutes Adam played on his own, while I dealt with the issue from nearby. After a few minutes had passed, I could see he was getting frustrated.

"What's wrong?" I asked him.

"All my money's gone," he said.

During my lapse in supervision, he had entered the world's virtual store and used all his game credits on a series of purchases for his avatar. These included a mini-UFO, a working toilet, and a snowman, all objects of great interest to him. He was disappointed to discover that he now lacked any credits to make further purchases.

"Sorry," I explained. "Once you spend all your game money, it's gone. You made your own choices on what to buy, remember."

"I know," he said. "My mom says stuff like that to me all the time in the candy store."

The game had reinforced one of Adam's important life lessons: spend your money wisely. But it also raised an important point for me — in mere minutes he had been able to spend all his virtual cash. Many unwary parents have discovered that it is equally easy for children to spend the real thing, with in-game purchases connected to credit cards.

It is worth noting, too, that few young children will be much excited by the sorts of educational games and apps that are just old-fashioned classroom worksheets disguised by rudimentary animation or encouraging messages. Design features are key to creating productive technological sources, such as videos and animations that inspire creative thinking, problem solving, and relationship skills. There are now many online games that students can play to help gain crucial skills such as numeracy awareness, problem solving, and critical thinking. Although such games are useful tools for older children who need reinforcement in specific skills, even younger children can easily distinguish between play and regular schoolwork; they will not likely engage in such programs in a creative fashion unless an educator or parent compels them to do so.

During one study, we provided a small group of children with iPads, each of which featured one game. Most of them were educational apps that promised parents worthwhile educational outcomes. Within minutes most of the iPads were discarded, as the children all gathered around one child, whose iPad featured a game which required children to engage in making ever more complex virtual pizzas. Teachers and parents can probably readily confirm children's predilection to be drawn to entertainment over education — they must judge the games and apps they use accordingly.

How to Assess Computer Games

The list of games and websites is endless; it changes constantly, as sites come in and out of fashion, become popular, and, in turn, are displaced by something new. Computer technology changes so quickly that a piece of software that was cutting edge for last year's class will be stiff and clumsy for this year's students.

It would be better, perhaps, for educators to think hard about a specific game or site, and ask, *"What will the children be getting out of it?"* If the answer seems to be nothing more than amusement, then it is time to move on. Otherwise, when choosing games or apps accessible to children, educators may be wise to adopt some of the following criteria:

- *Is the software fun?* If the children do not feel as if they are playing, it will not work on any level.
- *Is it suited to their ages and skills?* Just because it features a familiar cartoon character does not mean that it will be suitable.
- *Can the students understand the goals?* They need to feel a sense of accomplishment in the game environment if any other educational purposes are to be established.
- *Will the game allow pretend play?* If a game does not engage children's creativity and imagination in some way, it will probably have only limited appeal.
- *Can the software platform accommodate more than one child? Can they return to their own space in the game?* Most computer games allow a child to "save" his or her own character or accomplishments, something that children find valuable and important.
- *Will the game allow co-operation between students or small groups of students?* Co-operation is a vital skill in any group of young children and games that promote it will prove useful in a classroom setting.
- *Does the game get harder as the children become more experienced?* Better games expand and grow more difficult as the children get better at playing them.
- *Will the software allow a degree of trial and error?* Games that perfect this aspect will help children develop their intuitiveness.
- *Is the game too easy?* Games that constantly reward a child with compliments or credit not based on any real accomplishment are of little educational value.
- *Is the game too fast?* Many computer games rely on sophisticated animation and effects. Children often need time to think about and process tasks — the game should allow this.
- *What are the game's societal values? Does the game promote fairness, gender balance, and tolerance?* This can be a delicate area. Although few children's sites will be obviously flawed, games are often full of stereotypes that can easily go unrecognized. Educators need to be mindful of subtle messages buried in the game's characters and nuances.
- *Will children sympathize with and relate to the characters?* For example, few boys will wish to be seen playing a princess game (at least while under the scrutiny of their fellows), no matter how much fun it is. Similarly, a game based on a character associated most with younger children will be discarded quickly.

And, most important of all,

- *Have you played the game yourself?* No child, either in a classroom or at home, should be exposed to a game or website until the adult has thoroughly explored and tested it.

Teachers can provide guidance to parents and guardians about the value and use of digital media at home. For starters, tablets are part of daily life. Children who play with tablets can learn applicable skills such as coding and become active, rather than passive users by engaging in learning processes. In feature articles where parents are given a voice, it is reported that children who use tablets to enrich their learning have increased concentration, creativity, digital skills, and emerging literacy benefits.

Tablets are classified as "connected toys." They use technologies that respond to and interact with children, thereby allowing a program to personalize the app to the child. Although that capability may be good, children's apps are also notorious for containing hidden advertisements or extra levels that need to be charged to a credit card. It is important, therefore, that parents check the app on the tablet before allowing the child to play within it.

Copies of the line master on the next page can be given to students' families to consider.

Learning with Interactive Technology

Children do not generally distinguish between the value of screen play, such as that found on tablets and hand-held gaming devices, and real play. Teachers can make the best use of digital technologies when they combine them with other learning experiences. Below, Kindergarten teacher Carrie Collins shares how technology, including interactive whiteboards, can be combined with other teaching methods to enhance understanding of important concepts, such as letter-and-sound recognition.

Interactive Technology in the Classroom

Children learn when they have an opportunity to communicate, to question, and to reflect on their thinking, while seeing how they can make connections to what they already know, and one thing children already know is how to play. As a Kindergarten teacher, I encourage the development of thinking and learning skills by engaging children in meaningful and purposeful learning experiences that connect to their own lives. Nothing is more authentic to children than television and computers, which is why children as young as five years old easily adapt to using interactive whiteboards, such as the SMART Board.

Letter of the Week

One key concept for the Kindergarten student is letter-and-sound recognition. Students need to know not only how to say their ABCs, but also what sounds the letters make, what the letters look like, and how to print these letters. I dedicate a full week on one letter, using the "Writing without Tears" formula for letter development.

First, I model on chart paper how to form the letter, and my students use their fingers to draw the letter in the air on imaginary giant paper. I then demonstrate the sound the letter makes, asking my students to repeat the sound. We discuss the part of the mouth the sound came from and whether they use their teeth, tongue, or breath to make the sound. We brainstorm all the words that start with that letter of the week.

My students are then given playdough to form the letter. This is done in two different ways: the students roll out the playdough like a long snake and form the shape of the letter; or, usually on day two of our week, they roll the playdough flat and trace the shape of the letter into the dough with a finger or pencil.

Choosing Appropriate Apps: Advice for Parents

Choosing an app for a cellphone, computer, or iPad can seem daunting. There are so many that picking one or two to help children learn might seem impossible; however, choosing an app can be easy, if you keep these simple steps in mind.

1. Figure out what skill or experience you want the child to have. If you find an app you like, think about how it could encourage critical thinking skills or creativity. Remember that open-ended apps are more likely to offer creative opportunities.
2. If you find more than one app that suits your child's needs, discuss it with other parents or teachers. Consider how well the apps facilitate engagement, creativity, and the freedom for personalization.
3. Think about how the app can enrich an offline version of an activity or how both can work together to give the child the best creative experience. Some apps encourage children to use physical as well as digital objects during play. Other apps use motion-sensing technology for games that help children with spatial awareness. Still other apps teach children something about nature, gardening, science, or home life.
4. Ask yourself if the app will encourage co-operation between children. The best ones do. Storytelling apps, for example, help children craft their own narratives while interacting with other children writing stories. The apps allow children to learn to work together and find out more about each other.

Reading Apps: Reading apps for young children help them identify letter sounds, build words, and read words in ways that are engaging but not overstimulating. Apps that help children read should be well balanced between practice and play. They should also allow children choices to explore and grow.

Reading apps are usually interactive. Children can hear or repeat sounds to the screen, and practise reading words and stories out loud to help build their skills. When children use reading apps, parents are not excluded. Participating with children in their play to help them learn to read can be both fulfilling for the parents and meaningful for the children.

Points to Remember: The app should be something your child will enjoy. It also needs to be age appropriate and reflect your child's world. Be sure to check the app yourself for any hidden advertisements or potential credit card charges for higher levels of play. Remember, too, that no matter how popular apps are with children, they are not a substitute for real life. Children need time to play and learn offline — no digital technologies should ever replace those play opportunities.

Pembroke Publishers © 2019 *Invitations to Play* by Anne Burke. ISBN 978-1-55138-336-1

Continued from page 116

My students then have an opportunity to use our interactive whiteboard to write the letter on the board. I take this moment for assessment, using the recording feature. I record what my students write on the board, to determine if they are forming the letter properly. The students then click on their letter to hear its sounds. Eventually, this work leads into learning sight words, where my students play with the fridge letter magnets and the fridge magnet application on the SMART Board, dragging the letters to form letter combinations and words. This is often done in centres in combination with the playdough activities.

Exploration of the Self

Another key concept in Kindergarten is self. Using our interactive whiteboard and programs such as Kidspiration, Notebook, Paint, and Photo Story 3, I work with my students to create an "All about Me" portfolio which may include scanned or e-mailed pictures, drawn representations, and simple words. Parents are invited to contribute to their child's project, sharing pictures and audio files. I also have my students use a microphone and the Audacity program to comment on their lives, oftentimes pretending that they are news reporters. The children have grown up with television and computers, so completing their work using these media is both fun and meaningful for them.

Technology Skills as Side Benefit

The way I teach allows my students to use what they know to be a part of their everyday lives. Interactive whiteboards allow them to make observations and record characteristics, similarities, differences, and changes. They also let them create story webs and Venn diagrams, and classify materials, events, and phenomena (e.g., sort according to simple criteria such as color and size).

The side effect to this form of diverse learning is that my students can not only meet the desired learning outcomes in a cross-curricular manner but also acquire technology skills, including the proper use of a computer, keyboard, and mouse. They learn what and what not to do with a SMART Board — for example, not to use a regular pen or marker and how to touch the screen. They also learn how to use specific resources with the SMART Board, including a flatbed scanner; how to print; how to load a CD or DVD; and how to log on to the Internet.

— Carrie Collins

Makerspaces

Makerspaces are special centres, often found within schools, public libraries, and child-care programs, which provide do-it-yourself digital and engineering tools to allow children to build technological devices and complete projects. Makerspaces may also contain craft and art supplies and even basic woodworking materials. All resources are intended to encourage children to exercise creativity and take creative ownership of the material and digital worlds around them.

Makerspaces in early learning classrooms promote digital literacy, creativity, and learning. The technology within them can help children develop skills that they will need for future success. After all, children will face jobs and challenges later in their lives that are not even imagined today. Makerspaces promote the development of perseverance, curiosity, and innovation through technology. Some of them enable children to create functioning products, using tools and resources such as electronics, laser cutters, and 3-D printers. These spaces also sometimes offer digital "making," that is, the design and production of digital artifacts, texts, and products, with fabrication labs and other workshopping tools and materials.

A highly interactive, natural way to learn

There is no space more interactive than a Makerspace. Children embody the act of "making" and become physically engaged with their projects, trying and re-trying tactics; drafting and re-drafting plans; fixing what does not work; and striving to find a viable solution. In fact, children's lives lend themselves well to Makerspace creation. Children are inherently curious explorers, fascinated with the way their world works. Makerspaces incorporate that natural curiosity into classroom learning. Indeed, it could be argued that because Makerspaces deeply engage children's senses and attention, as would happen outside the classroom, they offer a natural way for children to learn.

An arts dimension

See the article "STEM vs. STEAM: Why the 'A' Makes a Difference" at http://www.edudemic.com/stem-vs-steam-why-the-a-makes-all-the-difference/. In the text box below, teacher-librarian Gina Brown outlines STEM or STEAM Makerspace challenges that students at Angus Morrison Elementary School, in Angus, Ontario, have undertaken.

There is an inherent bias in Makerspaces, though, in that, by design, a Makerspace needs digital technologies if it is to function. However, although many Makerspaces do incorporate interactive digital technologies, some Makerspaces also provide students with opportunities to learn through the arts, such as script writing, painting, and clay or fabric design. STEAM — Science, Technology, Engineering, Arts, Math — is an interdisciplinary learning system that was developed from the belief that traditional STEM learning did not provide enough creative thinking. STEM — Science, Technology, Engineering, Math — left out this key expressive component. It is realized more and more that young students benefit most from interdisciplinary learning that provides creative outlets. After all, today's young learners may encounter jobs, opportunities, and experiences that do not yet exist; they should be well equipped with the creativity, curiosity, and innovation that STEAM and that, by connection, Makerspaces provide.

STEM or STEAM Makerspace Challenges

The 21st century library can also be called a "learning commons." The teacher-librarians who run these commons purchase, catalogue, process, and curate books; promote reading and literacy; keep track of all the technology; run book fairs; and host authors and other engaging literary events, just as they did before this change in labels. But now, teacher-librarians also create Makerspaces in learning commons that transform the spaces from solely libraries to centres that foster problem solving, critical thinking, creativity, gender equality, empathy, responsibility, sharing, and exploration.

A learning commons Makerspace can be as simple or as complex as is needed. We have filled ours with non-consumables, such as Lego, blocks, measuring sticks, and cubes; and consumables, such as glue sticks, pipe cleaners, straws, old CDs, pompoms, duct tape, yarn, and any empty plastic containers or boxes we can find.

It is here in the learning commons that we began to promote STEAM challenges. Most of our STEM (Science, Technology, Engineering, Math) or STEAM — our county, Simcoe, has added the *A* for Arts — challenges began by using the Teachers Pay Teachers site, Pinterest, and some STEM books from Scholar's Choice. These activities have since evolved or been adapted and created through our partnership with other colleagues.

As teacher-librarians, we source out an appropriate read-aloud to begin these challenges. We create an anchor chart to describe the goal and the materials students will use to accomplish the goal. We also provide recording or reflection sheets for students in pairs if some of the students would benefit from drawing or writing down their plans, ideas, or end results. Next, we display all required materials on large open tables and in the Makerspace area.

Some of our most successful STEM/STEAM challenges include the following:

- Students had to create the tallest free-standing tower possible using only marshmallows and toothpicks — a great introduction or follow-up to their 3-D inquiries in class.
- Students designed a marble maze out of Lego and guided a marble through it by blowing the marble with a straw. This activity was so popular that we used it all the way up to Grade 7.
- During the holiday season, we developed a school-wide challenge. Each class or small group needed to create a holiday tree using ONLY recycled materials; an optional bonus task was to make the tree do a task. One small group created a tree using a Makey Makey circuit board that played music.
- The Winter Olympics encouraged students to create ramps from paper, books, blocks, and pennies to see which class could get the "skier" to jump the farthest.
- Our fairy-tale challenges have encouraged students to create bridges to hold the Three Billy Goats Gruff, towers for Rapunzel, beds for Goldilocks and the Three Bears, and homes to withstand the force of the Big Bad Wolf (a household fan).

We share the student learning by taking pictures and videos that we put up on the Seesaw app to share with parents. As a teacher-librarian, I also share student creations and experiences and video footage (with permission) through my school-wide Twitter account and blog.

— Gina Brown

Makerspaces as safe, inclusive places

All Makerspaces are about making things, but they vary much in appearance. The place could be a carpeted classroom corner nestled between bins of plastic bottle caps, string, glue, sequins, crayons, paper, scissors, or other items purchased from the discount store, donated, or brought from home. Or, it could be an entire room filled with more advanced hardware, such as sewing machines and 3-D printers. It could be as simple as a mindset established in a classroom for specific times of "making."

No matter what kind of Makerspace is created, it should have a low-risk, high-reward environment in which students feel encouraged to tinker, develop, and then share their creative products with others. Many Makerspaces encourage

Teachers and parents interested in Makerspaces can find many online resources, which provide designs, tool ideas, and suggested materials. Particularly popular are the apps and designs found on websites like Makey Makey which purport to be able to turn anyone into an inventor. For example, students can utilize these programs to design controllers that they use to play an online game.

Digital Children's Libraries

http://en.childrenslibrary.org/ (*Also an app*)

http://www.magickeys.com/books/

http://ufdc.ufl.edu/baldwin/juv/

https://www.oxfordowl.co.uk/for-home/find-a-book/library-page/

https://www.storylineonline.net/

http://www.read.gov/kids/

https://www.gutenberg.org/wiki/Category:Children%27s_Bookshelf

https://openlibrary.org/subjects/children#sort=edition_count&ebooks=true

collaborative projects that use anything from craft sticks and glue to e-textile (fabric that can conduct electricity) and 3-D printer programming initiatives.

Makerspaces provide students with hands-on, student-centred learning opportunities on a level learning field. Students with mental or physical challenges can take part. Children of different economic or cultural backgrounds, ages or genders, and levels of experience can all work either together or at their own pace and skill level. Makerspaces are not only inclusive, but also interdisciplinary, permitting multiple subjects to be combined. In Makerspaces, the learning process is as important as the finished product. Students take pride in their work and in presenting it.

Experiences described in this chapter speak to our need to be educators conscious of the choices we make and the offerings of particular games and sites. As educators, we must constantly seek positive ways to use technology, while reaching towards balance, taking into account the lives children lead at home and elsewhere. Technology and digital play will likely be a big part of children's lives, but it should be balanced with all the other elements in their play explorations.

7

English Language Learners and Play

As the primary occupation of children during their early years, play can integrate several aspects of the developing child, including the child's intellectual, cultural, social, physical, and creative inclinations. By its nature, play is free flowing, determined by the interests of the child. Children's play is improved if they have a wide variety of experiences to draw upon and the ability to communicate these experiences and ideas to others. The better their social skills, the better they are likely to communicate, and the more they will benefit from play.

Fostering Educational Play

The lighter the hand of the guiding adult, the more motivated and spontaneous the play is likely to be — this is really what it means to offer an invitation to play through an idea or an object. Researchers Rosemary and Peter Milne (1997) would go so far as to argue that "educational play in early childhood is neither play nor education. It is not play . . . if it is guided by an adult; neither is it educational in a rich sense if it lacks any adult guidance." In other words, when we use play to enhance children's education, we must be careful about what sort of play we are encouraging. For a child, play and fun are one and the same. If we are to maximize play's learning potential, we need to examine what children are doing when they play and then use this knowledge to further our understanding about learning in the classroom.

Recognizing the potential of symbolic play

In their early years, most children enjoy imaginative, or symbolic, play, where one thing is used to stand for or represent another. It can range from a child's simple imitation of adult actions — say, cooking and cleaning — to more elaborate fantasy scenarios, whereby household objects stand in for unicorns and castles. Symbolic play is vital for the development of representational and abstract thought. Early in their thinking, children rely on shared experiences. Through symbolic play they begin to process and understand events and scenarios that are in the past or the future, or are completely imaginary (Bruner, 1990).

The influential Russian psychologist Lev Vygotsky (2004) saw symbolic play as one of the first steps towards oral language and literacy — after all, languages are, first and foremost, a way of verbally representing the life we see around us. Vygotsky valued imaginative play, as it allows children to perform at a higher level; the context of such play is akin to the forms of knowing that children experience. It brings them to a state where they can reach beyond the concrete world of the here and now and, instead, play and imagine places, times, and scenarios not bound by their play space.

Literacy: Symbolic play versus structured programs

To take this into the realm of literacy development, we can look at the seminal work of Carol Taylor Schrader (see Schrader, 1999). She agrees with Vygotsky's theories, arguing that symbolic play is ideal for literacy development. Schrader prefers guided play scenarios, whereby the adult participates in the play, becoming part of the child's framework, but does not plan or otherwise direct it. The adult's role is to encourage the development of the play, with the goal being to expand its ideas, and to nudge the children to contribute as much as possible. Allowing children to direct their own play and to create their own rules while playing offers an authentic view into their thinking and a great opportunity for assessment.

Despite the value of symbolic play, the current trend in early childhood education is to emphasize earlier and earlier textual literacy, usually at the expense of playing. Play-based programs have been abandoned in favor of structured educational programs. Children are often passive participants in such programs, which see them as receptacles waiting to be filled with knowledge. Parents of children aged four to six are surrounded by media messages encouraging them to purchase all manner of early literacy toys and texts: all these toys and texts promise to have children reading flawlessly at a very young age. Spontaneous play is not part of the "schedule."

Using symbols in play and in literacy

Researchers such as Howard Gardner, however, believe that play is the very basis for literacy. Gardner's research has revealed that the creative processes inherent in play are the same that create literacy. This theory derives from the realization that a symbol represents something, perhaps an object, an event, or an idea. Words are also symbols. Whether we are adults or children, our thinking skills involve the manipulation of words — and ergo, symbols — as we use words, numbers, images, and notations to describe the world around us. The foundations of these manipulations are the real beginnings of literacy, *not* necessarily a child's first experiences with books.

Symbols are a real part of even the youngest child's play, even when not verbalized. Drawing, modeling-clay, painting, make-believe play — they all require the use of symbols. These symbols are, in turn, transformed into linguistic expressions, which then form the basis for oral and textual literacy.

It is interesting to note that during play, children can use complex forms of language. They use a larger vocabulary, which necessitates longer utterances than they might use in another context. These are important attributes of play for later literacy development.

Teachers may want to ask students to write a story using only symbols, such as emojis, small diagrams, even doodles — all of which will allow them to be more creative. Students will be excited about trying this kind of storytelling.

Ways to support vocabulary learning

In a classroom, it is helpful to have some guiding visuals and scheduled opportunities so that students can practise the vocabulary they have recently acquired.

- Displaying print materials that reflect student work helps students connect lessons to their English language learning and provides constant cycling and reinforcing of skills.
- Areas within the classroom library should be labeled and organized so that students can easily find the resources they are looking for.
- A language-related centre will provide a forum for students to tell and retell each other stories that they have read or heard, which helps reinforce language and vocabulary.
- Be sure to schedule time so that students can talk to one another. Having natural conversations will allow them to reinforce learned vocabulary and generate new vocabulary. It will also help students learn linguistic patterns and nuances.

Play, Literacy, and English Language Learners

Imaginative, interactive, and collaborative play situations and scenarios are ideal for children who are learning English as an additional language. They can provide a safe and engaging way for them to practise and use a new language. Children are very motivated to develop relationships with others. When engaged in play, they can develop language in a time and space that suits their needs rather than those of the classroom or household. Learning a language is not just about the technical aspects: social and cultural communication is also important in the language learning process.

Children from different cultural backgrounds come with different sets of experiences — the symbols they have developed to describe their worlds will differ greatly from those of native English speakers. As a result, we cannot assume that Western theories of play will apply to our English language learner (ELL) students. We should try to include teaching about symbols from the countries and cultures our students are from and allow students to compare and think about the similarities and differences in the symbols. Most of the theories about play we rely on come from Western studies, and our collective wisdom is dominated by our own experience in an English-speaking world. Some cultures value the role of play in children's lives; others do not. Adult participation in fostering play may or may not be required, encouraged, or apparent.

Educators who work with young English language learners need to be aware of their students' cultural differences and the cultural beliefs of the parents. Some ELL families will have just begun to settle in their new country. The values of the home country will be strong and will likely dominate parents' view of their children's education. Some customs will be modified, some will be cherished, and others may conflict with the educator's approach. Although such problems can be worked through, it is very helpful for educators to communicate with parents about mutual expectations.

ELL students learning language through play

Nonetheless, it is important to remember the findings of researchers such as Anca Nemoianu, who has made extensive studies of ELL students. Nemoianu (1980) convincingly demonstrated that children learn another language faster and with less effort during play, especially if they are trying to establish friendships with peers. Her research has been borne out by U.K. researchers Iram Siraj-Blatchford and Priscilla Clarke (2000) who also draw a link between the motivations of social play and children's ability to master a new language quickly.

Researcher Lily Wong Fillmore (1976) noted that children hear many phrases in a repetitive context during play, thereby making the phrases easier to learn. In my own experience, I saw this finding played out in my home community. I watched a vivacious four-year-old boy in my child's preschool go from almost zero English to a functional use of the language in just six months of companionable play.

Early childhood educators have a particularly valuable role in the play of English language learners. As they would for children with different economic backgrounds or physical abilities, they need to encourage all their students to cross these boundaries. All children need opportunities to express themselves through play, and professional educators can help make this happen. Educators should not shy away from becoming involved in such play, particularly where they see opportunities to support language development.

In the following feature, Julia Billard shares her first efforts to promote an appreciation of diversity and a respect for the many different cultures represented in her Kindergarten classroom.

One Teacher, 54 Students: Crossing Cultural Boundaries

Two weeks upon graduation, I travelled to Fort McMurray, Alberta, a town in the midst of an oil boom, bursting with new arrivals from across Canada and around the world. I walked into the District office on a Monday morning and by the next day I was given a full-time position as a Kindergarten teacher. I met with the principal and was given my class list — 54 students. "Wow" was my first thought, and my second was "I can't wait to meet the other teacher."

There was no other teacher. I was the only teacher for 54 five-year-olds.

I met with my 54 families — turns out that around 20 of them were ESL (English as a Second Language) students. Some of these students were fairly fluent in English, half spoke broken English, and one spoke no English at all. My classroom was like a garden salad of cultures, religions, and languages — and I was the spoon that had to keep everything mixing, blending, and moving. Many of my students' families had just moved to Canada, and neither parent nor child could really understand a word I was going to say.

I decided to make a conscious effort to keep placing myself in my students' situations. Would I be interested in listening to a story read in another language? How would I feel if everything I knew was uprooted and I had moved to this new English-speaking country where everyone talked and looked differently? Kindergarten was supposed to be fun and educational, but I couldn't even draw upon prior knowledge — I had none!

I wanted my students to embrace their home cultures and identities so in early October, we held a Multicultural Day. All my students wore or brought something that represented their culture. I wore a T-shirt from my home in Newfoundland, played some music from my own tradition, and taught the students how to dance a Newfoundland jig. Parents were also encouraged to join us, and many brought traditional foods such as samosas and Ukrainian perogies. The highlight of the day was when a very shy student, originally from India, taught the class a Bollywood-inspired dance.

I remember stopping to look around at my class that day, seeing everyone together, and realizing that it didn't matter if you were from Japan, India, the Philippines, Pakistan, Guyana, or Canada. Children are children, no matter where they are from in the world. They should be taught that their identity and culture make them unique; however, they also need to try new things, hear new music, and taste new foods. It was an entertaining day, but most important, everyone went home knowing more about and being respectful of different cultures. Even if some students didn't quite understand what I was saying, their smiles and laughter spoke volumes.

— Julia Billard

Scaffolding Play for ELL Students

The makeup of a given group of children will have a significant impact on the ultimate success of English language learners (just as it will have an impact on gender roles and socio-economic divisions). Educators can easily affect the makeup of these groups without becoming heavy-handed. We can readily encourage children who are fluent in English to mingle with those who are not.

Several simple classroom games particularly lend themselves to groups of children that include both ELL students and native speakers of English.

Picture Bingo: In this game, children match pictures held up by the bingo caller to the words on their bingo cards. To help them with the words, the bingo caller describes the chosen picture as a place, person, object, or whatever, thus making the game fair and informative for all.

Snap and Simple Card Games: Snap, to use one example, is a high-speed matching game, likely to be more popular among boys and competitive students, no matter their language proficiency. Old Maid and Crazy Eights are two more games students could play.

Snakes and Ladders: This simple board game requires no textual understanding other than the numbers on dice or a spinning wheel. With its sudden rewards and disasters, it appeals to children's sense of humor.

Jigsaw Puzzles: Encourage a group of children with different language abilities to work together on a puzzle. Choosing a puzzle of fewer than 100 pieces keeps young children interested and not easily frustrated. The key is for children to feel success.

Counting Games: Simple counting games — for example, how many children have long hair? how many are wearing something brown? — can be geared to suit children of all language abilities.

Matching Games: Almost all Western children have played matching games that involve turning over a series of cards to reveal which cards match. Cards that carry images, numbers, letters, or whatever can be chosen.

Games like these provide many opportunities for children to form sequences, ask questions, put labels on objects, take turns, and, most important, have fun in their new environment. They can be played in English, in another language, or in a combination of languages. Encourage children to make the language learning twoway — while the ELL students are learning English, invite them to share their first language with the other students.

Resources That Honor Diversity

Supporting an environment that honors diversity must be at the centre of planning for classrooms or early childhood education centres that have English language learners. Play resources, decorations, toys, and other materials all need to be chosen with this precept in mind. These resources, whatever they are, will often be the starting point for the children's spontaneous play or for play scenarios organized by the educator. We are talking primarily about the interior environment but can also encompass the playground and other outdoor spaces.

Here are some classroom ideas that can become the foundation for play scaffolding:

Home Corner: A home corner should be a space that encourages children to share family cultural practices, such as making dinner; or activities, such as holding a games night. Here, the various cultures represented by English language learners in the classroom are celebrated. Dolls make a simple way to demonstrate diversity, as do pictures, food labels in a different language, and cultural artifacts such as chopsticks. Aspects of the home corner should be chosen so as to encourage sharing by the English language learners, and curiosity and explorations by the native speakers of English.

It is important to take a careful look at the English resources that may be placed in the class library. For example, consider whether children of a different race are always illustrated in a rural or tribal setting — it is easy for stereotypes to become established among young children. Strive to avoid unnecessary stereotypes when choosing pictorial materials. Educators need to ensure that text materials provide a suitably diverse view of the world.

Class Multilingual Library: Thanks to the Internet, it is now possible to obtain texts from just about anywhere, or at least reasonable facsimiles of them. If resources allow, create a small multilingual library that incorporates the home languages of the class's students. Doing this will have several possible (and positive) outcomes. First, it demonstrates to the ELL students that despite the necessity of learning English, their home language is still important and valued. Second, it demonstrates to other children that a peer's language is not "wrong"; rather, it is as legitimate as English. Third, when the parents of ELL students see their own language validated, they may feel encouraged to become involved in the literacy pursuits of their children. In an ideal situation, books printed in several languages could be obtained, thus maximizing cultural exchange and multilingual efforts. These stories can, in turn, spur role-playing and other play scenarios.

Storytime: Storytime, a part of most early classroom experiences, can also be fine-tuned for ELL situations. Careful selection will allow educators to use books with minimal text, but highly evocative illustrations. While reading a story in another language may not be practical for all, it is something to consider. If nothing else, it would give English speakers some sympathy for the plight of the English language learner who arrives with little or no facility in English. As you would with any group of children, strive to engage children of different backgrounds, interests, and comprehension abilities. You may want to use some wordless picture books, as well. Doing so allows students to write their own story for the pictures or create a skit to tell the story. Stories can also help English language learners practise their language skills. Storytime is an informal way for ELL students to pick up language in a natural way; it is an easy, accessible way for all classroom learners to develop vocabulary.

Role-Playing: Some role-playing games lend themselves well to involving language speakers from different backgrounds. For example, a class could imitate different animals or act out simple activities such as household chores. Doing this would allow children with limited language abilities to participate fully in a play scenario.

Interactive Rhymes: Poems are a simple but effective way to assist English language learners. Finger plays such as "One potato, two potato" and "One, two, buckle my shoe" are good for teaching the concept of counting. Language is taught through repetition, and this principle can be extended to the classroom with ELL learners with great success. Hand-clapping rhymes such as "B-i-n-g-o," "Miss Mary Mac," or even "Say, Say, Oh Playmate" are popular with older children, as are tongue twisters and other funny and playful spoken-word games.

Photographs: Children like looking at photographs, which can provide visual representations of everyday life and be directly related to the students' families and community. Photographs can record memories and motivate children to talk about special events. Invite children to bring photos of themselves to class and talk about why they are significant. When talking about the photographs, they practise language and grow their vocabulary. In the case of photography show and tell, a picture is literally "worth a thousand words."

Photographs can also bring children together and help develop a classroom community. Children can find out more about their classmates. Photographs can show them how they are similar and also help them learn about differences to create understanding.

Teachers can create transparencies of each photograph so that all students can see them easily.

Music Games: Music is universal, and even the shyest ELL students may come to life when they hear a song in their first language. Music can be used in a variety of ways to enhance play scenarios for ELL students. Thanks to the Internet, a child-friendly listening post can be simply created, using MP3s that incorporate songs from many lands and languages. Simple play songs can help students to become involved in games: we may take for granted that everyone knows such songs as "Ring around the Rosie" or "London Bridge Is Falling Down," but they can play an invaluable role in involving ELL students with the wider classroom activity.

Promoting inclusiveness and a sense of belonging

A good idea is to encourage all learners to understand that people of different genders, races, and physical abilities have an equal role in our society. Examples include girls playing sports, men taking a role in domestic life, women working in a trade, and people of different cultures interacting. Looking through newspapers and local community bulletins would show children how everyone has an equal role when contributing to the community. Children can be encouraged to cut out pictures and newspaper headings that celebrate the roles people play.

It is also important to foster a sense of belonging in ELL students. Offer students the chance to teach the class about their culture or home country, and to teach some words of other languages they speak. Providing this opportunity can encourage a sense of belonging within the class and a sense of importance as the ELL students are the ones teaching their peers.

Using folk tales from students' cultures provides one way to be inclusive during Storytime. Folk tales help children expand on how they understand the world. The characters are easily identifiable, and the conflicts are easily understood and resolved. These stories can bring the class together to celebrate diversity. The conversations that stem from them will be meaningful: they often call into question how children solve their own problems or how they relate to others.

There are different types of tales to share: cumulative tales, pourquoi tales, beast tales, noodlehead tales, trickster tales, realistic tales, and fairy tales. Children love noodlehead tales, where a naïve and slow-witted character triumphs; or trickster tales, where a wily character outwits the unwary. All these tales, however, can reflect themes of cultural heritage and diversity and connect the students to past, present, and future generations of storytellers.

What to Consider When Involving ELL Students in Play

ELL students learn English better when they play with English-speaking children. Educators who promote this, either by leading or creating play opportunities and scenarios, would be wise to consider the following ideas:

- Certain children are outgoing and ready to take risks; others are not. Groups should include children of both types and offer opportunities to all.
- Children have different language abilities: some will learn quickly; others will take much longer.
- Motivation will vary widely, as will parental support.
- The play possibilities that the environment offers will greatly affect potential outcomes.
- Diversity in all its appearances, including through texts, visuals, and playmaking scenarios, is a necessary part of the ELL experience.
- ELL students need to see learning English as important, but without their home languages being diminished or dismissed.
- As much as possible, communicate with, reassure, and involve parents: they may not understand why or what play is doing in the classroom.
- Use of small speaking groups can help ELL students to feel more comfortable speaking English around their peers. By giving speaking topics, the teacher can guide the conversation and introduce new vocabulary or ask questions that require the students to express some deeper thinking.
- Be sensitive to different cultures. Take the time to learn from a student and his or her parents about their culture.
- When learning about another culture, keep an open mind to avoid any stereotypical thinking about a student's cultural background, knowledge, and ability.

Welcoming children who come to school with another language can be a challenge; however, it can be met through positive interactions. Keep in mind that language growth is stimulated when several of the children's interests are engaged. Having the home share in the child's school experiences can provide you with many points of connection. Some teachers, like Julia Billard, have created "Books about Me" with their ELL students so that the students can share their talents and

A list of website resources for teachers to use when developing diversity and play lessons appears in Recommended Resources (page 154).

Be aware that students from the same country (or general area) may speak different languages or have different cultures or beliefs.

interests with classmates. Through my classroom observations, I have learned that English language learners need to be able to trust their teachers, if they are to gain enough confidence to learn a new language. A key element in building this trust is the teacher's creation of many opportunities for children to feel successful right from the start of their classroom experiences.

Teachers of ELL students are often discomfited by their students' silence, but they need not be. Respect this silence as a time when the students are practising listening skills and gaining confidence in learning about language. Language is not just about the words we use to communicate but also about how to use words in certain situations. Some students may be more analytical in their learning (e.g., focusing on grammar and spelling, having difficulty asking for additional help); other students may be more holistic (focusing on the bigger picture rather than the fine details, more comfortable making mistakes and taking risks when communicating). Enabling children to play in small groups will provide valuable opportunities for them to develop the language and social skills they need for the early-grade classroom.

ELL Students: Individual Needs

It is essential to have an ESL specialist teacher on each individual education plan (IEP) team within a school. This teacher will provide valuable feedback on the needs, progress, and strengths of the ELL student, as well as support to the classroom teacher on how to address needs and help the student achieve within the curricula. The needs of ELL students will be met when teachers collaborate to modify and adapt programs to communicate more effectively with ELL students, and to foster a welcoming, safe classroom environment in which all students can learn effectively.

ELL students can be loosely grouped into four learning levels: the pre-beginner, the beginner, the intermediate learner, and the adept.

The pre-beginner — Little grasp of the English language

Pre-beginners need to be oriented to their environment before they can begin to speak, read, and write their new language. Learners at this stage can display a range of skills. When listening and speaking, some learners might be able to respond only to simple directions reinforced by visual cues, while others might respond to simple questions, songs, or familiar topics and understand basic instructions. Some children might be able to share their name and birth date but might not answer in complete sentences. Other children might use basic questions to seek information, imitate patterns, and identify names, objects, and actions.

When reading and writing, emergent pre-beginning students can recognize the alphabet and understand that English is read from left to right. They will also recognize words, songs, and stories familiar to them. They can write both upper- and lower-case letters and copy sentences easily. Some more advanced pre-beginners will begin to predict what happens next in a sentence and can identify the main ideas. When writing, students can, with assistance, draft short compositions, apply writing conventions, and copy whole sets of paragraphs or notes accurately.

The beginner — Beginning to use the English language

Beginners have a more complex understanding of English. They can understand slowly and clearly phrased spoken English sentences and paragraphs, even through the radio and telephone where speakers cannot be seen. They respond more readily to questions and begin to understand when and how to use humor. More advanced beginners actively participate in conversations and can respond to non-verbal cues such as body language. They also respond correctly to intonation variation, stresses, and pauses, and can pick out the main idea in oral presentations.

When reading and writing, the more emergent beginners apply vocabulary to stories, poems, and scripts, but make phrasing and rhythm mistakes when reading out loud. Beginners use the correct format to write lists, signs, letters, and journals, and use common words. Their sentences are short, however, because they apply only what they have learned in the classroom. Advanced beginners apply the reading strategies that they have learned to help them understand what a given word, sentence, paragraph, or story means. They can use the dictionary and thesaurus and understand key information from textbooks, using glossaries. When writing, advanced beginners can make notes with help and use conventional spelling. At this stage, beginners can write short responses in journals using the language learned in class; however, they need some help with the writing process.

The intermediate learner — Some grasp of the English language

Intermediate language learners have gained understanding of the English language but still need assistance in reading and writing. These emergent intermediate English language students can respond to others in conversation, to non-verbal signs such as body language, and to speakers even when they cannot see them. These learners actively begin and maintain conversations, speak clearly, and correct their own mistakes when they make them. More advanced intermediate learners, in addition to the skills learned by emergent intermediate learners, can respond to speech intonation patterns, use new vocabulary, follow more than one instruction in sequence, and identify important ideas presented in a variety of media.

When reading and writing, emergent intermediate learners can follow written instructions and describe characters, settings, and plot when discussing a story. They can understand grade-level text with little assistance. When writing, they can articulate their personal thoughts, collaborate with peers, and write independently in all subject areas. Advanced intermediate learners can scan text for new information and identify contextual vocabulary. They can predict, summarize, and make judgments based on what they read; they develop fluency when reading out loud. When writing, these students can create original compositions and reports on topics that are either academic or of personal interest. They vary their sentence structures and vocabulary and can form ideas into paragraphs that use the appropriate verb tenses.

The adept — Near age-level grasp of the English language

At this level, adept learners understand the English language at close to grade level, and they will expand this understanding throughout their school years.

These learners can participate in social and academic discussions and understand age-appropriate questions posed to them. They can also correct grammatical errors, create and present information to the class, and use idioms and colloquialisms easily. More advanced learners at this level can use grade-level vocabulary when giving academic presentations in class and take notes from lessons (if provided with an outline). These students are able to respond to English used in a variety of settings and can employ teasing, irony, flattery, humor, and sarcasm. They can explain a point of view. They have gained confidence in their ability to speak clearly and fluently in front of a large group.

When reading and writing, emergent English learners at this level can respond to instructions that have been written down and retell stories that they have heard. The texts they choose to read for pleasure are much like those that their peers are reading. Students at this level can write short original compositions and use proper punctuation most of the time. More advanced adepts can parse meaning from unfamiliar texts and use strategies to acquire new and challenging vocabulary. They can identify elements within a story. The reading materials they choose are at a level comparable to what their peers choose in both skill and scope.

Combining Language and Content

The differences between the emergent and advanced learners at each level is the difference between content knowledge acquisition and language content acquisition. Learning content and language together is a more effective teaching strategy than learning content and language apart. When teaching ELL students, educators should build language instruction into their content-area lessons so that students learning the new language can gain both academic and cognitive language proficiency.

Benefits of drawing on students' first languages

Teachers can help enhance the learning of English as a second or other language by taking advantage of as much first-language support as possible (e.g., from parents, peers, volunteers, dictionaries, and books). Promoting a positive attitude towards other cultures and languages helps create a healthy classroom community. By extension, teachers should find and use activities in the classroom that promote the sharing of other cultures and languages and encourage students to use and share other languages they speak. (In the early learning stages, teachers should encourage them to write in their first language.) They thereby promote multiculturalism. Teachers of ELL students should allow the classroom to reflect multicultural diversity through use of signs, books, posters, and more. They should consider the academic and emotional needs of both ELL students and native speakers of English and provide additional individual support to ELL students while they are building relationships with their classmates.

Playful ways to promote content understanding

Teachers of ELL students need to be well organized and provide clear classroom rules and activities. They should also consider placing the ELL students where the students can both see and hear them during instruction; the students benefit from being able to observe other students, too. Finally, as with all students, teachers must ensure that both parents and students understand the rules, regulations, and expectations of the classroom and school.

When teaching a science lesson on weather and the seasons, for example, you might ask students to draw pictures of the sun, moon, stars, rain, clouds, thunder, and snow. If children do not understand these words in English, ask for their help to identify the words in their own language. Then, to help reinforce what the words actually mean, you could use nursery rhymes such as "**Rain, rain**, go away, come again some other day" or "Cold and raw the north wind doth blow, Bleak in the morning early, All the hills are covered with **snow**, And the winter's now come fairly."

To help strengthen students' understanding of concepts in nature, you could use riddles. Ask: "What is in the sky? It's not a cloud. It's not a bird. But in the winter and summertime it keeps us warm." Students can hold up the pictures that they drew of the sun. (See https://owlcation.com/academia/Teaching-pre-school-English.)

If the classroom has developed play centres, you could use directional language to help ELL students practise their listening and comprehension skills. For example, assume that the classroom has play centres modeled after a museum, a zoo, a candy store, and a café. You could give short, clear directions for students to follow. "Go to the museum. Turn right. Pet the tiger in the zoo. Buy a lollipop in the candy store. Turn left. Sit down in the café." And so on. (See https://hubpages.com/education/TPR-in-teaching-pre-school-English.)

Watch your language

Teachers are well advised to be conscious of their own speaking and use of language, especially around ELL students. Students will benefit if you slow your speech, speak clearly, enunciate well, and speak loudly enough that every student can hear you. Modify the language you use, as well. Talk in shorter, less complex sentences, avoid slang words, and repeat or paraphrase main ideas. Use more visual learning, too, as in diagrams, pictures, non-verbal communication, facial expressions, and body language. Reintroduce new vocabulary words in multiple contexts and in multiple curriculum areas. Repeat ideas as necessary so that all students may be successful, and model corrections when students make language errors. If possible, use a student's first language to check for understanding; if not possible, check for understanding frequently. Provide additional time for ELL students to process and respond to questions or inquiries.

All these measures will help your students' language learning grow.

8 Building Citizenship through Child Play

As children play in their physical environment, they learn how to use their world to advantage. One of the greatest aspects of true free play is that it allows children to learn and to take risks in a safe environment. Safe learning, in turn, builds self-confidence and teaches fair play, turn-taking, co-operation, and more. For example, on a playground's climbing equipment, children can test their physical limits in a relatively risk-free environment, exercising those skills until they have mastered them.

> *When my own son was mastering his sliding technique on the small playground near our house, his constant shouts of "Watch me again, Mommy," were not just about showing off. He was testing his abilities and challenging his physical limitations. His repeated actions — and my many, many affirmations — were all part of the long process of building his self-confidence. From such free play, children learn to take risks, solve problems, and expand their horizons.*

Many parents exercise confidence-building tactics instinctively, so most children come to school with a great sense of accomplishment upon which teachers can build. The main influencers of a child's social skill set are the parents and other adults in the child's life. We want to create a positive reflection of children's abilities; in turn, self-confident learners contribute to building a classroom where collaborative learning flourishes. Children will develop positive attitudes that encourage them to become active citizens and partake in collaborative decision-making. Active citizenship that is responsive to the needs of our society begins when teachers engage children in collaborative learning activities; skills developed from such activities draw upon children's understanding of social responsibility and prompt children to think critically about how their actions affect the well-being of others and the community.

Helping children to understand who they are and how they can contribute to making a healthy community will build their social, cognitive, and emotional well-being. When children can explore their feelings, talk about concerns, and express their opinions in an early years' classroom, they form positive relationships, and that enhances their self-confidence and self-esteem. Children need to become skilled in how they use language to communicate ideas and express emotions — doing so will help build a collaborative classroom and contribute to a healthy community.

What they learn through observation influences how children adopt social skills. The way key adults in their lives respond to others has an impact on how children will handle themselves in similar situations to come. Social norms such as holding the door open or chewing with mouth closed are unconsciously observed and absorbed by children. These habitual behaviors in daily life become the main examples from which children learn.

We must remember that children understand their world based on what they have learned in the home. For example, many children in our society learn at an early age about the tooth fairy, a mythical being who exchanges money for baby teeth. While English-speaking Canadian children probably accept this belief, when they go to school, they may encounter other beliefs. For example, in many Latin American countries, baby teeth are exchanged by a little mouse. Other cultures have no traditions about baby teeth, and children from such homes may find the whole thing ridiculous. The home provides a foundation of cultural reference points; whether they intend to or not, schools inevitably offer much broader perspectives.

Other areas of child development such as cognition, language, and emotional development are strongly connected to social skills. During their early years, in their own social and cultural contexts, children form concepts about who they are and how they relate to the world around them. Children are helped to develop a positive self-image, show independence, and self-regulate within the context of the home and in early years' classrooms. Through the development of interpersonal skills, they learn to communicate their opinions and thoughts. A positive self-image provides a child with the confidence and independence that bring forth critical and creative skills; these, in turn, lead to social competence and emotional intelligence. Children learn to take responsibility for themselves and others.

This chapter looks at what it means to develop a child's positive understanding of self and other people; it also recommends skills you may wish to build in children. The activities shared here will help to create a collaborative learning classroom that moves students closer to understanding the importance of citizenship.

Developing Understanding of Community

Children become aware of what it means to be a part of a community at a young age. They understand that a community can be a playgroup, their classmates, or a family. Community has both social and cultural aspects; it is a huge part of the way we communicate and create meaningful experiences in our lives.

One way in which children interact with one another is through musical experience. This allows them to feel that they are part of a group and it gives them joy. The soul is stimulated through music, thus helping children come to terms with their emotions. Music in all its diversity allows for children to focus on a tune that relates to their emotional mood.

For children, engagement in a community gives them a chance to communicate, to learn, and to contribute to something that matters to the world outside their own limited experiences. Playmaking creates many opportunities for this sort of learning to be explored. Here is an example.

Each morning, in Sue-Ann Carter's Grade 1 class, the children share their Pokémon cards. Because they find the nuances of the proper game too complex to grasp, they have created a simple version of the game, which involves trading cards with similar images. For the several weeks in which the game maintains their collective interest, the children call the daily game sessions the "Pokémon Club," loudly proclaiming their membership. In other words, they have formed a community, one based on their creation and enjoyment of a card game.

Girls, on the other hand, have formed communities based on Shopkins, the response to the toy industry that produced Pokémon cards for boys. Shopkins are part of a trend that produces toys with tactile surfaces — Squishies and slime. Small collectibles based on grocery-store items, they each have a face, name, and personality. They have been at the top of many Christmas toy lists.

Shopkins appealed to the girls in different ways. Lilly and Bella were particularly interested in the different finishes that some Shopkins have — how glittery, shiny, or squishy the characters were. Other children ranked the characters by how rare they were. Some girls liked the lines of Shopkins that had articles of clothing, appliances, or accessories associated with them. A number of girls wore Shopkins T-shirts.

Girls found Shopkins in categories such as sweets and bakeries especially appealing. They would spend many recess or lunch hours pretending that they were in a bakery or sweet shop, trading Shopkins as part of their play. Girls would also draw their favorite Shopkins or even create their own from their imaginations. They would trade these drawings, both created and re-created, as part of their play.

Being a part of something means having special beliefs and values. Teaching young children to become aware of the world in which they make meaning requires that they develop skills in which their voices and actions have both meaning and consequence at the same time. Becoming a good citizen requires the development of communication skills, expressions of viewpoints and opinions, listening and empathy with others, and situations being shared. In a classroom, learning what it means to be a citizen may be as simple as children perceiving how they are to behave.

If children understand how positive choices contribute to a school community and how negative choices lead to misunderstandings and conflict, they will be better able to appreciate what it means to contribute to the classroom and communities in which they live. Establishing classroom rules supports this effort. When doing so, teachers should ask their students to come up with a list of the rules they believe the class should follow. This involvement will help to develop a sense of autonomy within the class and foster a greater sense of responsibility to obey the rules that students helped devise.

In addition to this, there needs to be a discussion about the difference between *fairness* and *equality*. It is important that students develop an awareness and understanding that being fair does not always mean that every student gets the exact same thing (equality). *Fairness* means that all students get what they require in order to meet their individual needs. That is the desired goal.

Building Blocks to Community

Once children have a sense of community and some empathy for others, they can build on these foundations. They can begin to understand the organization of their community, the dynamics of families, and how people can all contribute to our democracy. Although these concepts are somewhat weighty, they are well within the grasp of even very young children. They must, however, be offered to them in a fashion to which they can relate.

School communities strive to have children see themselves within a larger world and what that means within a diverse society. When children develop an appreciation for the differences found in others, they can more readily accept others' opinions and respect viewpoints that may be different from their own. As young learners develop socially, cognitively, and emotionally, they must come to understand that everyone within a community has rights and responsibilities. Accepting and celebrating the many cultures that may be represented, as well as gaining a basic perception of equality, are also important. When teachers foster the development of emotional maturity and healthy self-image in children, it helps children make positive choices and celebrate the diversity in the world: they first come to accept themselves and then learn to take responsibility for each other.

Identity is formed at an early age, and a name is probably the first way in which the child defines who he or she is. Children need to understand that the names of others are representative of who they are, too. Names are chosen through practised customs — they may have personal, cultural, or religious significance. Using children's first names is a good way to build respect and to introduce positive ideas about identity and self-identification within the classroom. (See "Working with names" in Chapter 3.)

Engaged learners, responsible citizens

To evolve into socially and morally responsible citizens, children need to acquire the skills of active and engaged learners. Building such foundations on their sense of what community and responsibility mean places them in a world where they can act with confidence and commitment, with an understanding of the positive difference that they can make. A child who possesses strong social skills is most likely to have an easier progression through childhood into adulthood than someone without those skills.

Creating a peaceful school with a student body whose members are respectful of one another is part of the growth of a healthy community of learners. On a playground, all of us have heard the names that children give to others who may be different or have seen how some children are excluded for reasons unknown to us. At the same time, teachers and parents often have cause to notice how refined young students' sense of justice is. We need to be able to build on this sense so that children may become aware that their actions affect the well-being of others — even in a global sense, it is important to instill in children the recognition that they have a role to play in caring for the earth. Through learning how to think critically and solve problems, children come to understand that through their own efforts, they can contribute to the creation of a community.

Classroom play on collective responsibility

One of the best ways to enhance children's sense of responsibility for their own community is through a play-acting game, What Happens Next? The children are given a scenario and are asked to play-act what should happen next. After one or two children act out a given scenario, the rest could be invited to share their opinions, something that builds their critical thinking and problem-solving skills. Innumerable teachable moments can arise through use of drama and skits, and these can be used to show multiple sides of the same situation (various points of view or opposite behaviors).

A key element of each What Happens Next? scenario is that some clear moral or responsible action is indicated. As the children will usually figure out the best course of action, the teacher need not pass judgment on the outcome. The scenarios can be simple for younger children or more elaborate for older ones. Here are some suggestions:

- As a child, you find a brand-new toy on the school playground.
- You start eating your lunch, only to discover that it is someone else's.
- Everyone in class is going to get into trouble for something you just did.
- You accidentally broke the sink in the washroom.
- You saw someone littering outside the school.

Sharing and Its Foundations

Play shapes children's beliefs about how to act in society: children learn by doing it and by observing it. The age of three is when a child's social skills can be applied in real-life situations. At this age, children who possess the proper language and social skills will take turns and play co-operatively with others by their own accord. When fatigue comes into play, however, these skills seem to crumble and often a tantrum ensues. One key thing for them to learn is how to share. Classroom activities that require children to take turns, share ideas and values, respect others' feelings, and know how to conduct themselves all lead to and are part of harmonious relationships. We see these values in classrooms when children can share their ideas in a collaborative group setting. Often, though, young children need to understand what their needs really are before they can share within the classroom.

The Roots of Empathy program is another way to help children develop a deeper awareness of their feelings and teach them how to show empathy and caring for others. This positive international program promotes the development of good citizenship and parenting over the long term. It focuses primarily on children ages 5 to 13.

While visiting one classroom, I watched a group discussion in which the classroom teacher talked about the differences between wants and needs. Creating a chart with the children, the teacher discussed needs such as food, water, and a home, as opposed to wants such as toys, holidays, and video games. Doing this provided a good opportunity for the children both to acknowledge and see their own priorities laid out in front of them. The children showed an awareness of their own feelings and began to understand the feelings of other children in the group.

Discussing their way into community

Children work naturally together and enjoy sharing their understanding and perceptions of what they observe. Learning communities are developed through collaborative group discussions where problems are identified and explored. Everyday occurrences — the cancellation of a gym class, a lack of supplies, a spilled drink — are problems for which children can easily provide collective solutions. Modeling language that points to problem solving will help children to understand problems. Eventually, they can be invited to form a sharing circle and give their opinions on how to address the problems.

The discussion that follows provides an example of proactive problem solving that promotes community building.

From a Problem to the Building of Trust

In her Grade 1 class, teacher Mernia Reid expresses concern over a recess-break safety issue.

Mernia: Friends, we have a problem. Does anyone know what the problem is?

Luke: I know . . . I know. Kate slipped on juice that was on the floor.

Mernia: Yes, you are right, Luke. We are sorry, Kate, that you were hurt. Of course, we do not want anyone else to get hurt. We need to find a solution to our problem. It is not anyone's fault, but it is everyone's responsibility to keep each other safe. What do you think we should do?

At this point, Mernia asks the children to engage in problem solving. The children make suggestions: "I think we should only have juice boxes because they do not spill as much," voices Hilary, followed by Darren, who says, "I can only bring my drink in my thermos." Eric shares his feelings: "My mom says they are a waste because the box is more garbage."

Mernia decides that a list of possible ways to solve the problem may be the best solution. The children share their solutions.

Sit at your desk when you eat or drink.

Don't walk around.

If you spill something, clean it up or get help from the teacher if you need to.

Be responsible and tell the teacher you had a drink accident.

Try to use a plastic container for less waste.

Remind someone who has made a spill to clean it up and help that person do it.

Mernia offered some silly suggestions to make the situation more playful — these the children easily rejected.

Through resolution of this classroom problem, the Grade 1 class set a routine for how to deal with what might have become a bigger problem, that of a student being hurt. Students agreed that the rules and the set routine were important, and all children felt that their ideas had been heard. Taking turns and sharing while seeking a solution to the problem also helped build trust in the community.

Making Responsible Decisions

The building of a collaborative learning environment requires children to develop some knowledge about how their decision making affects others. Ideas like this, as well as more esoteric ideas, such as consensus, are relatively easy to demonstrate in a playful fashion.

I remember one game my own Grade 2 teacher used — it is as useful today as it was then. She asked everyone to stand next to their desks, extend their arms, and then slowly swing their arms around in a circle. Then, she prompted half the class to step forward and we did the swinging again. In the crowded classroom it was only seconds before children began banging into each other. Our clever teacher then asked us to decide who would be allowed to swing their arms around as much as they liked and who should sit down out of the way. The ensuing debate was lively and perfectly illustrated to us what taking personal responsibility and forming a consensus felt like.

There are many other ways of achieving this, as well.

Illustrating what *consensus* means through a showing of hands or use of thumb up or down helps children to visually connect with decision making in a personal way. Count hands or thumbs and announce the numbers in a decision. The topic need not be important, but it should be something of interest to the children.

Inviting children to voice their thoughts and opinions is important. "It is cold today," a teacher might say. "Should we dress warmly and go out, or stay inside? What do you think?" Or, something even simpler: "Will we make paper chains or draw pictures to decorate the classroom?" Displaying decisions through either charts or other visual aids, such as pictographs, records the different opinions that have been expressed. It also acknowledges everyone's voice.

Helping children to weigh the positive and negative effects of their decisions asks for them to look at the pros and cons. To use the examples from above, the teacher could subtly create a wider debate: "But if we go outside, some of us will be cold . . ." "We don't have enough scissors for everyone to make chains, so some of us will have to wait for a turn." The idea is to get the children thinking about their impact on the lives of others.

Using Play to Create Collaborative Communities

Creating a working community depends on young children coming to understand the importance of their contribution to the group, which involves sharing and agreeing on a vision. The concept of collaboration (or *co-operation*, as it is apt to be termed in a preschool setting) is important for play-based activities. Play often depends on collaboration.

It is simple for a teacher to provide opportunities for collaborative free play, which builds these skills. Most primary teachers will already be familiar with some of the examples given here:

Blocks and Construction Toys: Instead of working on their own projects, children could be encouraged to create a collective construction — maybe a tower or wall across one end of the classroom. Each child would have several blocks or pieces to contribute to the construction as he or she saw fit.

Board Games: More so than many board games, Snakes and Ladders teaches children patience and the importance of obeying collective rules. Older children can play with the basic concept. Perhaps they could invent their own rules for the game: they might decide that every time someone lands on a ladder all the pieces move up, no matter where they are. Children are often intrigued by their ability to alter the supposed reality of the game and by the fact that their collaboration is required for it to work.

Jigsaw and Map Puzzles: Puzzles are ideal for creating play-based co-operation, though they probably work better with some children than others. One interesting variation is to give each child a set number of pieces and then have the children take turns placing the pieces. Doing this enforces a certain degree of give and take among the children. It enhances their collaboration.

Inviting students to co-operate

On one occasion, I observed how a Junior Kindergarten teacher, Lisa Deon, created moments of collaborative play in her suburban classroom. I saw how she used language to invite the children to share in the work: "I think we need to tidy up the centres. Who will help with the drama corner? And the blocks? Thank-you, Julia and Sienna. My, with us all working together, we will have this done in no time." When they were finished, she complimented the most helpful, saying, "You are great helpers — this is why we work so well together."

In helping students to build community as a cohesive group, Lisa often asks individual students to seek solutions by co-operating with others. Over and over again, and in various ways, she returns to some key questions:

- Can everybody help in some way?
- Can you help them become a part of the play?
- How are everybody's listening ears?
- What did you decide to do first?
- Who is good at this part? Can you help him or her?
- Has everyone had a turn? How can we include everyone?
- What do you like about what you did here?
- What can you improve?

Children are born with the need to feel a part of a community. The playgroup, daycare centre, or classroom will provide their first opportunity to take part in a community outside their own families. To develop as confident individuals, they need to feel that they are respected, that what they say is valued, and that their presence is important to the whole. Children who understand that they are a part of a community will take positive risks and can balance their decisions, which, in turn, leads to problem solving and learning to collaborate.

Connecting Children to the Environment through Play

Due to urbanization, curriculum shifts, and parental concerns, there is less time during the school day for children to play outside. Yet, authentic experiences in the natural world provide many opportunities to use all forms of play that contribute to children's positive development. When children play outside, they make friends and energize their imaginations. Playing outdoors has also been shown to relax aggressive behavior, reduce the risks of obesity, and calm anxiety. Beyond that, it connects learning to enjoyable experiences, which, in turn, encourage even more physical activity and lifelong learning.

Having children connect to the wider world in the ways we make decisions is a necessary part of this process. Protecting the environment is a huge concern for society at large, as well as our schools and communities. One way that outdoor play promotes sustainability is through empathy. Students learn to respect all living things and to think about the impact of their actions before stepping on a bug, breaking tree branches, or lifting salamanders out of brooks, for example. They learn how to touch small insects and worms with care. By extension, students who show empathy towards other creatures and their environment are likely to show empathy to their peers and teachers, thus helping to create a global, sustainable community.

Books can help provide introductions to outdoor play through empathy. *Gummytoes* by Sean Cassidy tells the story of a frog that wants people to admire him. When he is caught by some children and stuck in a jar, he wishes he were back in the woods alone. Because the book is told from the frog's perspective, children connect with the character and relate what he feels to other animals (see https://thecuriouskindergarten.blog/category/outdoor-classroom-2/). This helps children consider the impact that their play has on the natural world around them.

Although concepts such as sustainability may be complex, creating play scenarios in which they are explored is relatively easy. Some of the games are very simple. One favorite of many teachers is a smelling game (which can be adapted to teach other concepts, as well). The teacher selects several natural substances — for example, cut grass, wildflowers, mud, tree bark, fresh fruit, and sawdust. Students take turns blindfolding one another and then trying to identify the various substances. The game is fun and sensory, but it also teaches children about the variety of life.

A similar play scenario asks students to gather leaves from their immediate neighborhood and then make tracings or rubbings from them. Even very young children will be intrigued by evidence of the wide variety of natural life around them.

Building gnome homes is one way that students can combine architecture, nature, community, and sustainability. Students use objects such as bark or moss, rocks or leaves, and flowers or acorns to construct temporary, artistic, lean-to structures for "gnomes." They must problem-solve to create these homes, using only the materials around them. Working without adhesives, students develop fine motor skills and learn to balance objects on top of one another.

As a class, students can build a community of these homes. Because the homes are built for another creature — a gnome — students develop empathy. By learning to get along with "neighbors" and share building sites and materials, students grow closer and strengthen the classroom community. Finally, by creating the homes out of objects from the natural environment, students can learn to choose materials whose use will not have negative effects on the environment around them.

Nature walks and acoustic walks are other ways in which students can develop a connection to the environment. On a nature walk, students can collect pieces of nature, such as twigs, leaves, or stones, and then use these in an art project. On an acoustic walk, students can take notes about all the different things they hear in their environment, such as birds chirping, cars humming, dogs barking, and doors opening or closing. After this walk, they can write a story which connects all the sounds into one storyline.

Simple classroom tasks can be turned into interesting games. After lunch, one teacher asked her students to put all the waste on their desks. The children then had to decide what could be recycled, what might be composted, and what would have to go to a landfill. Older students can participate in an environmental footprint quiz. First, they challenge one another to remember all the ways they use energy and resources in a given day; second, they assess whether they are doing their bit to conserve (e.g., using juice boxes or reusable containers, walking or taking a bus to school, eating fruit or a packaged snack).

Recycling household objects for arts and crafts is hardly new to most teachers and students, but if students are challenged to find new uses for things and new things to make use of, fresh impetus can be added to the activity, which becomes play. I have seen this game played out in a Grade 2 class as part of a school's Earth

Day activities. Some of the children came up with ingenious uses for discarded objects: picture frames made from cereal boxes, matching games made from old catalogue cut-outs, and juice-box dolls were just a few.

Introducing environmental concepts

Concepts such as global warming and water conservation are difficult to explore through play scenarios, but they can be introduced through games. Many teacher manuals and websites suggest play-acting and tableau games to create awareness of these problems; however, these may or may not be appropriate and realistic for a given class or group of children. Teachers can use simple games to at least introduce these concepts. For example, solar energy can be explored by placing wet cloths in various places around the classroom — the sun's power as a drying agent will be easily established. Drying substances such as fruit in a sunny spot will have the same effect.

Although the dangers of pollution do not readily lend themselves to conventional play, basic concepts can be introduced to children through play scenarios. These scenarios prepare students for more serious education in the higher grades. Children will be quite conscious of being preached to, however, so play scenarios should rely on simple playful concepts and not veer into strict instruction.

The early years' classroom environment builds the foundations for citizenship through the exploration and collaborative learning offered through playmaking. Children learn to see themselves as unique and valued contributors to the workings of the classroom community. Playmaking and the effort of solving everyday classroom problems help them to work together and understand that everyone has rights and responsibilities. An early introduction to the democratic processes at work in problem solving prepares young learners to embrace social responsibility and understanding of others and differing viewpoints. Although these concepts may be perceived as complex for the young learner, citizenship truly begins with the basics of taking turns, respecting others and their thoughts, understanding and feeling empathy for others, and choosing to become actively engaged.

9

Playful Learning through Music

A group of young children responding to music is a source of amazement. No matter how busy the children might be with their own projects, when a teacher puts on some recorded music, they respond almost immediately — bending, marching, dancing, clapping, hopping, and singing along. This interactive play-making is ideal for literacy development.

All children have a natural affection for music. Even infants respond to soothing melodies from their caregivers, while toddlers will engage with all different kinds of music and make their own music when given the opportunity. Children will use music for socializing, for entertaining themselves and others, even for expressing their ideas and emotions.

And music can do much more than entertain. Study after study has illustrated how interacting with music, even at a very young age, helps children build their cognitive abilities, intelligence, and brain power, expanding and creating neural pathways that are key to whole worlds of early learning. More specifically, children's phonemic awareness and capacity for reading skills, as well as aural language development, are all enhanced by even rudimentary musical interactions (Chau & Riforgiate, 2010).

Early childhood programs should all include music and sound exploration. Playful approaches to music exploration are key to the development of young children's music appreciation.

Benefits of Music to Children's Development

Music can make a significant contribution to three major areas of early childhood development: children's physical development, cognitive development, and social development.

Physical development

As children move from infancy through the toddler years and into early childhood, they are constantly developing physically. Their balance, co-ordination, and fine motor skills are critical aspects of this development. While they move through their play, they are learning to use these functions. Music — which encourages dancing, hopping, clapping, and other more complex movements — can contribute to this process.

Cognitive development

Early learners and toddlers make great strides in cognitive development. They are still developing speech, thinking, and memory. Music can contribute to all these areas, and has been demonstrated to enhance language proficiency, spatial reasoning, and temporal reasoning. It also increases understanding of moods, emotions, and other cultures, and via musically inspired movement, children can gain greater sensory awareness of the world around them.

Social development

During these early years, a child's social development moves from an entirely ego-based stage into shared play and early friendships and co-operation. Music making and music play can be positive shared experiences. They offer great opportunities for children to develop socially.

Experiencing Music

Young children encounter and engage with music in a variety of ways:

- Engaging with music leads to the discovery of sounds and how they can be made and manipulated.
- Music can stimulate movement or direct involvement.
- Music can spark imaginative and spontaneous responses.
- Because of the collaborative nature of music, involvement can enhance children's social development.

Discovering sound — Instruments

Exploring sounds and how they can be made provides a wonderful source of discovery for children. While older children can be taught how to play real musical instruments, younger children will enjoy making music in a wide variety of ways. Regardless of instrument availability, both children and their teachers will enjoy making instruments of their own. When creative minds are at work, simple craft supplies can be turned into wonderful music-making devices.

Shakers: Shakers are the simplest instruments to make, and even the youngest learners can assist in their construction. Rudimentary shakers can be made from paper cups and pebbles, covered in paper and secured by tape or rubber bands. More complex shakers can use paper-towel tubes and seeds, with paper covering both ends. Larger paper tubes can be turned into rain sticks, an instrument fascinating to children of all ages.

Drums: Drums require a surface more or less resonant and sturdy enough that children can strike it over and over again in order to make a noise. Drums need not be expensive or elaborate. Every child-care centre seems to have a surplus of plastic food containers, and these can be adapted. Other drums can be made from food containers and heavier boxes. Old pots and pans can be repurposed as drums, while makeshift tambourines can be constructed using two paper plates containing a few seeds or pebbles.

Wind Instruments: Making wind instruments can be very interesting and engaging for children. The simplest versions are just lengths of flexible hose, with makeshift horns constructed of paper cones. Older children can make pan pipes from plastic straws cut into different lengths and glued together; younger children will take great pleasure in the sounds that can be made by blowing across a plastic bottle.

Xylophones: Xylophones seem complex, but almost anything resonant can be turned into a simple xylophone or thumb piano. Gluing craft sticks of different lengths across a small box will create a xylophone which is quite serviceable, and thumb pianos can be made with old boxes and rubber bands of varying thickness.

An effective lesson or unit can also be built around the origins and history of these instruments. Many simple instruments have their origins and antecedents in Indigenous cultures or have arrived with immigrant communities. Children are often interested in the roles these instruments play — for example, for religious ceremonies and community demonstrations. Educators and the children in their classes can playfully explore these cultures through the instruments and the roles they play in people's lives.

All these instruments can be combined into noisy, but fun ensembles; or, children can just experiment with their instruments together or individually. Basic music concepts such as rhythm and groove (rhythmic feel) can even be explored, as children play the instruments in repeated patterns, or in concert with each other. Children will often already know the tunes of simple nursery rhymes, and these can be used to guide the instrumental explorations.

Discovering sound — Singing

Singing is often a part of early learning centre activities, but in the wider context of music and play, it can offer many other playful explorations, too. These explorations can be subdivided into several subcategories: sound production, collective singing, and song making.

Chances are most children sing without even thinking about it; however, exploring the way they make sounds can open many doorways for sensory play. Singing teachers often utilize exercises that teach their students how to enunciate vowel sounds, elongate notes, and scoop and slur phrases. Although these music concepts may be too advanced for most children to grasp, the actual sounds are not complicated, and children take great delight in learning that they can control their own voices. Similarly, whistling, tongue clicks, lip smacking, and other aural creations are all music and can contribute to children's appreciation of sound.

Singing together

Singing together provides an excellent way for children to socialize, improve relations with their peers, and explore their sensory environment. Children's singing is naturally spontaneous and often exuberant, so the goal is not musical perfection so much as participation and involvement. The best songs are simple, repetitive, and clever, with strong, memorable phrases and choruses. Rhythms should be simple and catchy, and the melodic range should not be difficult for anyone. Songs can be selected to reflect seasons, history, and cultural explorations, or, they can fit the current theme in a classroom or at a daycare centre. Many children's songs, such as "Ring around the Rosie," are quite old or are traditional. These songs can lead to many imaginary or historical excursions within the learning setting.

Simple songs in other languages can be an amazing way to introduce children to other cultures or give ELL students an opportunity to contribute to group activities. The lyrics to songs like the French "Frère Jacques" or the Spanish "Hola, Hola" are easy for children to master and provide a playful learning experience.

Song making to familiar tunes

Song making is an interesting way to encourage play and creativity. Even educators often believe that song making is complex when, in fact, it can be quite simple. Caregivers can encourage children to alter the words of songs to fit their own circumstances, making them more resonant and fun. These song variations can even include parodies and playful references to children's own situations. Song making works best when the children already know the melodies and rhythms, so using well-known and familiar songs is best. For example, the rhyme scheme and melody of "Take Me Out to the Ballgame" can be transformed into something like this:

> Let's go out to the playground.
> Let's line up in the hall.
> Boots, snowsuits, and mittens, please.
> We don't want any fingers to freeze . . .

Or, you might adapt the children's favorite, "Twinkle, Twinkle, Little Star":

> Twinkle, twinkle, candy bars.
> How I want you from afar.
> Sitting in the candy store.
> I'm not allowed to eat some more.
> My mom says I need heathy food.
> Candy puts me in bad moods . . .

The possibilities are endless, limited only by the children's imaginations.

Another approach to song making is to utilize moniker songs — children's songs that use many personal names. Songs like "The More We Get Together" allow educators to include all the children's names in various verses, thereby encouraging both participation and self-identification.

> The more we get together, together, together,
> The more we get together, the happier we'll be.
> 'Cause your Emma is my friend, and Obie is your friend.
> The more we get together, the happier we'll be . . .

Discovering sound — Movement

Movement is children's first and most instinctive response to music. For caregivers and early learning facilitators, it provides an excellent opportunity to engage children in music and musical experiences.

Children's propensity for movement is well known. Much current theory about movement, music, and play was inspired by the German composer and educator Carl Orff. Orff believed that music was an elemental part of human behavior and could be used to awaken and begin developing movement in all children. He devised several teaching tools to encourage this process. Orff's work provides the foundation for many of the games and exercises that young children do in pre-Kindergarten music programs.

Early learning centre programs can use simple versions of these exercises to create their own opportunities for musical movement. The idea is to enable children to dance, march, clap, and explore a whole range of sensory movements, all inspired by the music they hear and create. These movements should, in turn, enhance spatiality, sensory development, listening skills, fine motor skills, and social interactions. Orff and his later theorists always emphasized one point, however: the musical movements should be fun!

Orff believed that the starting point for music in early learners should be body percussion. As young children are becoming aware of their bodies and the spaces around them, simple human percussion such as clapping and stomping in time can teach key music concepts such as time and rhythm, while offering enormous fun. These movements can be combined with marching in a circle, basic dances, or any other movements that let children express themselves and react to the music without injuring anyone.

Getting Started on Musical Adventures

Early learning educators and caregivers can guide children in their musical adventures by following a series of informal phases.

The first should focus on *exploration*, using movement, singing, or musical instruments as described earlier. Instead of just playing a CD and letting everyone jump around, the idea is to encourage the children to explore sounds and interact with one another, using music as the source material. Subtle questions can guide activities: "Could we make a circle, where everyone makes a different sound?" "What sorts of sounds can we make using just these two sticks?" "Can you clap your hands in different ways?"

Children love *imitation*, which can be a great way to introduce music concepts and ideas. Musical games, such as creating a line of echoes, clapping and stomping in repeated patterns, or marching down a hallway in time can teach children about listening and rhythm, and promote socialization.

Improvisation means building on earlier patterns and sounds to expand beyond the guided processes. With improvisation, the goal is never to produce something listenable so much as it is to encourage playful iterations of sounds. Essentially, educators and caregivers can encourage children to listen to the patterns and sounds they create, and then alter them to make something different. Very quickly children's natural imagination and curiosity will take over. The result will invariably be a cacophony; however, learning that they can alter their sensory environment is a powerful moment for children. "Old MacDonald Had a Farm" is a fun repetitive song, but when children are encouraged to change the rhythm, the words, and the tempo, it will turn into something else.

Ultimately, the goal of these processes is *creation*, in which children take sounds, movements, and instruments and spontaneously create music of their own. These creations can be simple and personal, or they could involve the whole group depending on the children's proclivities, the educator's ambition, and the space and materials available. Many children love to perform and organizing simple concerts can be a wonderful way for them to establish confidence and self-esteem. Giving them creative agency is also a powerful lesson. Simple poems, rhythmic pieces, and movement can be combined in an infinite number of ways, all of which allow children to experience the sounds they are making as real music: something that can be made, but also received and enjoyed by an audience.

Building a Play-Based Music Program

Using the strategies outlined above, an early childhood education centre can easily create its own play-based music program. Activities should be organized so that children can experience sound and music in several different ways, through singing, movement, and improvised instruments, and by exploring the world of sound around them. Collaboration and creativity may need more subtle guidance, but children should feel agency in their own creations and be given opportunities to collaborate with, perform for, and listen to one another.

The Music Centre

The goal of the centre is to provide opportunities for playful creativity and sound making. When creating the Music Centre, be sure to keep in mind how music influences child development, the purpose of musical play, and simple musical concepts. The Music Centre could include songbooks and lyric sheets, children's recordings, and enough craft supplies to make simple instruments. The emphasis should be on offering children lots of things to do, not on having them listen passively to CDs. Instruments that can be shared and that encourage further discoveries are invaluable. Opportunities for children to play together are always exciting.

This chapter concludes with a feature about how two teachers, Lindsay Cadieux and Renee Young, involved their students in storytelling through music, movement, art, and words.

Telling Stories through Music

Music has always been a huge component of our Grade 2 program. It's amazing how motivated and excited the students become when you add a little music into their day — from singing songs to implementing routines, to playing music to teach a new concept or idea, to using it to practise self-regulation. The transformation that a student undergoes when you add in music is astonishing.

An original script on a familiar character

This past year, our students re-created stories with puppets and masks. We modeled this process first and the students eventually began to try it on their own. Because of this interest, we decided to create a Pete the Cat musical — Pete the Cat was one of their favorite book characters. We took a Pete the Cat book, rewrote it as a manageable script for the students, and added in music at appropriate times. Our students were inspired and began to create their own movements to illustrate it. The beauty of this was that it enabled all our learners to be fully involved.

Combining music and literacy had an unexpected benefit for a number of students with special needs, too. While they did not want to take part in some learning experiences, this musical integration gave them the confidence to participate in a capacity developmentally appropriate and on par with their peers.

A movement drama to end an inquiry

An ongoing inquiry in our classroom had been about seeds and planting. Using a workshop technique and Lois Birkenshaw's book, *An Orff Mosaic from Canada*, we worked with *The Little Brown Tulip Bulb*, a movement drama, to discover the needs of plants. We spent time exploring simple percussion instruments and discussed how each instrument's sound made the students feel. We then discussed how we could use these instruments to make the sounds of the wind, the rain, the sun, and the tulip bulbs, with each student making suggestions and explaining the reasons behind their suggestions.

The class also explored how the music made them want to move, prompting students to devise movements to represent these environmental concepts. Using chiffon scarves in different colors and masks that the students made, we re-created the story through music, movement, and words.

The students were very excited to share their performance. Many of them attempted later to incorporate the musical ideas into their own plays. As with our Pete the Cat musical, this process allowed all our learners to be successful and contribute in a creative and engaging way.

— *Lindsay Cadieux and Renee Young*

References and Resources

Bandura, A. (1977). Self-efficacy: Toward a unifying theory of behavioral change. *Psychological Review, 84*(2), 191–215.

Baroody, A. J., & Dowker, A. (Eds.). (2003). *Studies in mathematical thinking and learning. The development of arithmetic concepts and skills: Constructing adaptive expertise.* Mahwah, NJ: Lawrence Erlbaum Associates.

Barton, D., & Hamilton, M. (2000). Literacy practices. In D. Barton, M. Hamilton, & R. Ivanic (Eds.), *Situated literacies: Reading and writing in context* (pp. 7–15). New York, NY: Routledge.

Bertram, T., & Pascal, C. (2002). What counts in early learning. In O. N. Saracho & B. Spodek (Eds.), *Contemporary perspectives in early childhood curriculum* (pp. 241–256). Greenwich, CT: Information Age.

Booth, D. (1998). *Guiding the reading process: Techniques and strategies for successful instruction in K–8 classrooms.* Markham, ON: Pembroke.

Branscombe, N., Burcham, J., Castle, K., & Surbeck, E. (2014). *Early childhood curriculum* (2nd ed). New York, NY: Routledge.

Bronson, M. (1995). *The right stuff for children birth to 8: Selecting play materials to support development.* Washington, DC: National Association for the Education of Young Children.

Bruner, J. (1978). The role of dialogue in language acquisition. In A. Sinclair, R. J. Jarvella, & W. J. M. Levelt (Eds.), *The child's conception of language* (pp. 241–255). New York, NY: Springer-Verlag.

Bruner, J. (1990). *Acts of meaning.* Cambridge, MA: Harvard University Press.

Bruner, J. (1996). *The culture of education.* Cambridge, MA: Harvard University Press.

Canadian Council on Learning [CCL]. (2007). Survey of Canadian attitudes toward learning. Retrieved from http://www.ccl-cca.ca/CCL/Reports/SCAL/2007Archives

Canadian Language and Literacy Research Network. (2009). *National strategy for early literacy: Report and recommendations* (D. G. Jamieson). London, ON: Canadian Language and Literacy Research Network. Retrieved from http://en.copian.ca/library/research/nsel/report/report.pdf

Chau, C., & Riforgiate, T. (2010). *The influence of music on the development of children* (Unpublished senior project). San Luis Obispo, CA: College of Liberal Arts, California Polytechnic State University.

Clay, M. M. (1991). *Becoming literate: The construction of inner control.* Portsmouth, NH: Heinemann Educational Books.

Clay, M. M. (1993). *An observation survey of early literacy achievement.* Portsmouth, NH: Heinemann Educational Books.

Clay, M. (1993). *Reading recovery: A guidebook for teachers in training.* Portsmouth, NH: Heinemann Educational Books.

Clements, J. (2018). *Teaching English by the book: Putting literature at the heart of the primary curriculum.* New York, NY: Taylor and Francis.

Davidson, J., & Wright, J. L. (1994). The potential of the microcomputer in the early childhood classroom. In J. L. Wright & D. D. Shade (Eds.), *Young children: Active learners in a technological age* (pp. 77–91). Washington, DC: National Association for the Education of Young Children.

Dyson, A. H. (2003). *The brothers and sisters learn to write: Popular literacies in childhood and school cultures.* New York, NY: Teachers College Press.

Edminston, B. (2007). Mission to Mars: Using drama to make a more inclusive classroom for literacy learning. *Language Arts, 84*(2), 337–346.

Elkind, D. (2001). *The hurried child: Growing up too fast too soon* (3rd ed.). Reading, MA: Addison-Wesley.

Erickson, E. (1963). *Childhood and society* (2nd ed.). New York, NY: Norton.

Fillmore, Lilly Wong. (1976). *The second time around: Cognitive and social strategies in second language acquisition.* (Doctoral dissertation). Stanford, CA: Stanford University.

Galda, L., Ash, G., & Cullinan, B. (2000). Children's literature. In M. Kamil, P. Mosenthal, P. D. Pearson, & R. Barr (Eds.),

Handbook of reading research: Volume III (pp. 361–379). Mahwah, NJ: Lawrence Erlbaum Associates.

Gelman, R., & Brenneman, K. (2012). Moving young "scientists-in-waiting" onto science learning pathways: Focus on observation. In S. Carver & J. Shrager (Eds.), *The journey from child to scientist: Integrating cognitive development and the education sciences* (pp. 155–169). Washington, DC: American Psychological Association.

Graves, D. H. (1994). *A fresh look at writing.* Portsmouth, NH: Heinemann Educational Books.

Gray, P. (2008, November). The value of play I: The definition of play gives insights. *Psychology Today.*

Gregory, E., Long, S., & Volk, D. (2005). Syncretic literacy studies: Starting points. In E. Gregory, S. Long, & D. Volk (Eds.), *Many pathways to literacy: Young children learning with siblings, grandparents, peers and communities.* New York, NY: Routledge.

Griffiths, R. (2005). Mathematics and play. In Janet Moyles (Ed.), *The excellence of play* (2nd ed.). Buckingham, England: Open University Press.

Hall, K. (2000). A conceptual evaluation of primary assessment policy and the education policy process in the republic of Ireland. *Compare: A Journal of Comparative and International Education, 30*(1), 85–101.

Hall, N. (1987). *The emergence of literacy.* Portsmouth, NH: Heinemann Educational Books.

Harste, J. C., Woodward, V. A., & Burke, C. L. (1984). *Language stories and literacy lessons.* Portsmouth, NH: Heinemann Educational Books.

Heath, S. B. (1983). *Ways with words: Language, life and work in communities and classrooms.* Cambridge, England: Cambridge University Press.

Hewes, J. (2006). *Let the children play: Nature's answer to early learning.* Montreal, QC: Early Childhood Learning Knowledge Centre.

Howe, A., & Davies, D. (2005). Science and play. In Janet Moyles (Ed.), *The excellence of play* (2nd ed.). Buckingham, England: Open University Press.

Kiefer, B., with S. Hepler & J. Hickman. (2007). *Charlotte Huck's children's literature* (9th ed.). New York, NY: McGraw-Hill.

Kress, G. (2003). *Literacy in the new media age.* London, England: Routledge.

McLeod, S. A. (2018). Lev Vygotsky. Retrieved from https://www.simplypsychology.org/vygotsky.html#evaluation

Miller, E., & Almon, J. (2009). *Crisis in the Kindergarten: Why children need to play in school.* College Park, MD: Alliance for Childhood. Retrieved from Alliance for Childhood website: http://www.allianceforchildhood.org

Milne, R., & Milne, P. (1997). *Marketing play: Using marketing strategies to explain the benefits of play approach in early*

childhood education. Melbourne, AU: Free Kindergarten Association.

Moll, L., Amanti, C., Neff, D., & Gonzales, N. (1992). Funds of knowledge for teaching: Using a qualitative approach to connect homes and classrooms. *Theory into Practice, 31*(2), 132–141.

Morrow, L. M., & Rand, M. K. (1991). Promoting literacy during play by designing early childhood classroom environments. *The Reading Teacher, 44*(6), 396–402.

Moyles, J. R. (1989). *Just playing: The role and status of play in early childhood.* Philadelphia, PA: Open University Press.

Mustard, J. F. (2006). *Early child development and experience-based brain development: The scientific underpinnings of the importance of early childhood development in a globalized world.* Washington, DC: Brookings Institution.

National Council of Teachers of Mathematics. (2000). *Principles and standards for school mathematics.* Retrieved from the NCTM website: https://www.nctm.org/Standards-and-Positions/Principles-and-Standards/

Nemoianu, A. M. (1980). *The boat's gonna leave: A study of children learning a second language from conversations with other children.* Amsterdam: John Benjamins.

Papatheodorou, T., & Moyles, J. R. (2012). *Cross-cultural perspectives on early childhood.* Thousand Oaks, CA: Sage.

Parr, T. (2003). *The family book.* New York, NY: Little, Brown Young Readers.

Piaget, J. (1962). *Play, dreams, and imitation in childhood.* New York, NY: Norton.

Piper, T. (2003). *Language and learning: The home and school years* (3rd ed.). Upper Saddle River, NJ: Merrill.

Play England. (2018). *Adventure into sport: Evaluation report.* Retrieved from http://www.playengland.org.uk/wp-content/uploads/2018/07/Adventure-into-Sport-Evaluation-report.pdf

Play Wales. (2018). *Playing and hanging out* [video]. Retrieved from http://www.playwales.org.uk/eng/playinghangingout

Roskos, K., & Christie, J. (Eds.). (2000). *Play and literacy in early childhood: Research from multiple perspectives.* Mahwah, NJ: Lawrence Erlbaum Associates.

Schrader, C. (1990). Symbolic play as a curricular tool for early literacy development. *Early Childhood Research Quarterly, 5,* 79–103.

Shedlock, M. L. (1951). *The art of the story-teller* (3rd ed). United States: Dover.

Siraj-Blatchford, I., & Clarke, P. (2000). *Supporting identity, diversity, and language in the early years.* Buckingham, England: Open University Press.

Smilansky, S. (1968). *The effects of sociodramatic play on disadvantaged preschool children.* New York, NY: Wiley.

Smilansky, S. (1990). Socio-dramatic play: Its relevance to behavior and achievement in school. In E. Klugman & S.

Smilansky (Eds.), *Children's play and learning: Perspectives and policy implications*. New York, NY: Teachers College Press.

Street, B. (2000). Literacy events and literacy practices. In M. Martin-Jones & K. Jones (Eds.), *Multilingual literacies: Reading and writing different worlds* (pp. 17–30). Amsterdam: John Benjamins.

Sutton-Smith, B. (1971). The playful modes of knowing. In N. Curry & S. Arnaud (Coordinators), *Play: The child strives toward self-realization* (pp. 13–24). Conference proceedings of the National Association for the Education of Young Children, Washington, DC.

Teale, W., & Sulzby, E. (Eds.). (1986). *Emergent literacy: Writing and reading*. Westport, CT: Ablex.

Vygotsky, L. (1978). *Mind in society*. Cambridge, MA: Massachusetts Institute of Technology.

Vygotsky, L. (1988). The genesis of higher mental functions. In K. Richardson & S. Sheldon (Eds.), *Cognitive development to adolescence*. Hove, England: Erlbaum.

Vygotsky, L. S. (2004). Imagination and creativity in childhood. *Journal of Russian and East European Psychology, 42*(1), 7–97.

Wells, G. (1999). The zone of proximal development and its implications for learning and teaching. In *Dialogic inquiry: Towards a sociocultural practice and theory of education* (pp. 313–334). Cambridge, England: Cambridge University Press.

Wenger, E. (1998). *Communities of practice: Learning, meaning, and identity*. Cambridge, England: Cambridge University Press.

Books Reflecting Gender Balance

Goblinheart: A Fairy Tale by Brett Axel

The Adventures of Tulip, Birthday Wish Fairy by S. Bear Bergman

Postcards from Buster: Buster's Sugartime by Marc Brown

They She He Me: Free to Be! by Maya Gonzalez and Matthew Sg

I Am Jazz by Jessica Herthel (and Jazz Jennings)

The Boy with Pink Hair by Perez Hilton

Jacob's New Dress by Sarah and Ian Hoffman

Large Fears by Myles E. Johnson

Roland Humphrey Is Wearing a WHAT? by Eileen Kiernan-Johnson

My Princess Boy by Cheryl Kilodavis

Julián Is a Mermaid by Jessica Love

Daddy, Papa, and Me by Lesléa Newman

A Fire Engine for Ruthie by Lesléa Newman

Heather Has Two Mommies by Lesléa Newman

Mommy, Mama, and Me by Lesléa Newman

Sparkle Boy by Lesléa Newman

It's Okay to Be Different by Todd Parr

When You Look Out the Window: How Phyllis Lyon and Del Martin Built a Community by Gayle E. Pitman

And Tango Makes Three by Justin Richardson

Pride: The Story of Harvey Milk and the Rainbow Flag by Rob Sanders

The Boy & the Bindi by Vivek Shraya

From the Stars in the Sky to the Fish in the Sea by Kai Cheng Thom and Kai Yun Ching

Resources to Use When Developing Diversity and Play Lessons

http://www.oxfordseminars.ca/esl-teaching-resources/lesson-plans/

http://theconversation.com/teaching-artists-creative-ways-to-teach-english-to-immigrant-kids-42588

http://www.english-4kids.com/grade2.html

https://www.teachingenglishgames.com/primary

https://www.eslkidstuff.com/Gamescontents.htm

http://iteslj.org/c/games.html

https://teach-english-in-china.co.uk/8-activities-primary-esl-classes/

https://www.teachingenglish.org.uk/article/motivating-speaking-activities-lower-levels

https://www.edutopia.org/article/resources-for-teaching-english-language-learners-ashley-cronin

Other Sources and Reading

Barefoot Computing. (2014). Abstraction. Retrieved from https://barefootcas.org.uk/wp-content/uploads/2014/10/Abstraction-Concept-Barefoot-Computing.pdf

Canadian Children's Book Centre. (2018). Road Trip Reading Club printables and activities. Retrieved from http://bookcentre.ca/road-trip-reading-club-printables-activities

Clements, J. (2017). *Teaching English by the book: Putting literature at the heart of the primary curriculum.* New York, NY: Taylor and Francis.

Davies, D., Jindal-Snape, D., Collier, C., Digby, R., Hay, P., & Howe, A. (2013, April). Creative learning environments in education — A systematic literature review. *Thinking Skills and Creativity, 8,* 80–91.

Donahue, M. Z. (2017). The ten best STEM toys of 2017. *The Smithsonian Magazine.* Retrieved from https://www.smithsonianmag.com/innovation/ten-best-stem-toys-2017-180967316/

Duron, L. (2018). 8 books that teach kids about the fluidity of gender and the importance of acceptance. Retrieved from Brightly https://www.readbrightly.com/8-books-that-teach-kids-about-the-fluidity-of-gender-and-the-importance-of-acceptance/

Gadanidis, G., Brodie, I., Minniti, L., & Silver, B., (2017, April). Computer coding in the K–8 curriculum? [Research monograph #69]. *What Works? Research into Practice.* Retrieved from http://www.edu.gov.on.ca/eng/literacynumeracy/inspire/research/Computer_Coding_K8_en.pdf

Goodreads. (2018). Children's books that break gender stereotypes. Retrieved from https://www.goodreads.com/list/show/34011.Children_s_Books_that_Break_Gender_Stereotypes

Hands On as We Grow. (2018). Blocks of fun! 47 block activities for preschoolers. Retrieved from https://handsonaswegrow.com/lots-of-blocks-activities/

Hatch, M. (2014). *The Maker movement manifesto.* United States: McGraw-Hill Education. Retrieved from http://www.boerneneshovedstad.dk/media/1332/maker-movement-manifesto-sample-chapter.pdf

Hoyte, C-A. (2018). Gifts activities. Retrieved from the Canadian Children's Book Centre website: http://bookcentre.ca/programs/td-grade-one-book-giveaway/gifts-activities

Hoyte, C-A. (2018). Caramba activities. Retrieved from the Canadian Children's Book Centre website: http://bookcentre.ca/programs/td-grade-one-book-giveaway/caramba-activities

John, S. (2018, April 4). The tech toys that secretly teach my kids coding skills. *The Strategist.* Retrieved from http://nymag.com/strategist/article/stem-toys-educational-toys.html

Kumpulainen, K., & Gillen, J. (2017). *Young children's digital literacy practices in the home: A review of the literature.* Retrieved from http://digilitey.eu/wp-content/uploads/2018/02/WG-1-Lit-Review-04-12-17.pdf

Literacy Apps. (2017). How to choose apps. Retrieved from http://literacyapps.literacytrust.org.uk/how-to-choose-apps/

McDonnell, A. (2016, October 20). Read-alouds for outdoor learning. The Curious Kindergarten [Blog]. Retrieved from https://thecuriouskindergarten.blog/category/outdoor-classroom-2/

Nieuwmeijer, C. (2013). *The role of play in music education for young children.* Utrecht, Netherlands: HKU University of the Arts.

Orff, C. (1973). Orff-Schulwerk: Past and future. *Orff Institute Yearbook.* Cleveland, OH: American Orff-Schulwerk Association.

Patten, K. (2018). 37 children's books that crush gender stereotypes. Retrieved from the Midlife Mamas website: https://themidlifemamas.com/childrens-books-that-defy-gender-stereotypes/

Reading Rockets. (2010). Environmental print. Retrieved from http://www.readingrockets.org/article/environmental-print

Reading Rockets. (2017). Nature: Our green world. Retrieved from http://www.startwithabook.org/booklists/nature-our-green-world

Run Wild My Child. (2017, October 24). Beautiful children's picture books about nature. Retrieved from http://runwildmychild.com/beautiful-nature-books/

White, J. (2018). Flower shop: Dramatic play center. Retrieved from the Play to Learn Preschool website: https://playtolearnpreschool.us/flower-shop-dramatic-play/

Acknowledgments

This book, in the making for many years, captures my work with teachers in Canadian classrooms. I wish to thank and acknowledge the following educators for their contributions: Gina Brown, Karen Pragnell, Renee Young, Lindsay Cadieux, Jane Lloyd, Sue Ann Carter, Mernia Reid, Julia Billard, Sandra Quinton, Trevor Mackenzie, Leslie Murray, Kelly Ellis, Karen Norman, Cecile O'Brien, Susan Barron, Debbie Toope, Carrie Collins, Toni Doyle, Jenny Temple, Susan Walsh, Nancy Pelley, Keri-Lynn Lannon, Janelle Lake, Karen Keough, Lisa Deon, Carol Sanchez, and Leslie Murray. Honoring what children know and offering many invitations to play, they are celebrated in this book for their dedication to new knowledge, young learners, and shared classroom pedagogies.

A special thank-you goes to research assistants Abby Crocker, Kayla Ellis, Emily Hancock, and Jennifer Kennedy.

And to my mentor David Booth: I am in awe of and inspired by you always.

Index